D1251306

SHIPWRECKS
OF GREAT BRITAIN AND IRELAND

In the same series
Cornish Shipwrecks. The South Coast
by Richard Larn & Clive Carter
Cornish Shipwrecks. The North Coast
by Clive Carter
Cornish Shipwrecks. The Isles of Scilly
by Richard Larn
North Wales Shipwrecks
by Ivor Wynne Jones
Devon Shipwrecks
by Richard Larn
Goodwin Sands Shipwrecks
by Richard Larn

SHIPWRECKS
OF GREAT BRITAIN AND IRELAND

Richard Larn

387.5
Lar

David & Charles
Newton Abbot   London   North Pomfret (Vt)

810844

To my Mother

British Library Cataloguing in Publication Data

Larn, Richard
   Shipwrecks of Great Britain and Ireland.
   1. Shipwrecks—Great Britain—History
   I. Title
   387.5'0941   VK1282.G7

   ISBN 0–7153–7491–5

© RICHARD LARN 1981
All rights reserved. No part of this
publication may be reproduced, stored
in a retrieval system, or transmitted,
in any form or by any means, electronic,
mechanical, photocopying, recording or
otherwise, without the prior permission
of David & Charles (Publishers) Limited.

Filmset in Monophoto Plantin by Latimer Trend & Company Ltd
and printed in Great Britain
by Redwood Burn Limited Trowbridge and Esher
for David & Charles (Publishers) Limited
Brunel House   Newton Abbot   Devon

Published in the United States of America
by David & Charles Inc
North Pomfret   Vermont 05053   USA

CONTENTS

(Picture credits are given in captions and the extensive
selection from the author's collection are credited *(RLC)*)

Methought I saw a thousand fearful wracks;
A thousand men that fishes gnaw'd upon;
Wedges of gold, great anchors, heaps of pearl;
Inestimable stones, unvalued jewels,
All scattered in the bottom of the sea.

Shakespeare, *King Richard III*, Act I Scene IV

PREFACE

Throughout history the ship has predominated as man's largest and most versatile form of transport. The ship has also been the most important single instrument of exploration, trade and war. Had early man not dared to venture afloat—perhaps astride a floating log, then eventually aboard a raft on the open sea—the world would still be in its primitive state. The importance of ships towards man's progress on earth has therefore been incalculable, possibly more so than any other single device. Without ships we would have continued to believe that the world was flat, and the native occupants of at least half the world's continents would have remained in ignorance of the other's very existence. England would never have experienced the oppression of invaders, nor profited by their culture. Spain would never have found its 'funnel of gold' in the Americas, or other European nations the wealth of the East. In fact, without ships the course of history as we know it would have taken an unimaginable turn.

Ships and sailors face the elements together, each dependent on the other for survival. It is therefore not surprising that an affinity bordering on affection exists between ships and the men who work them.

With so many moods and faces, inevitably the sea brings moments of disaster, and a countless number of vessels lie strewn across the ocean floor and around these shores. Proportionately, no island in the world has a worse record for shipwrecks than Great Britain. Just how many wrecks there have been is pure speculation, since no-one knows, not even

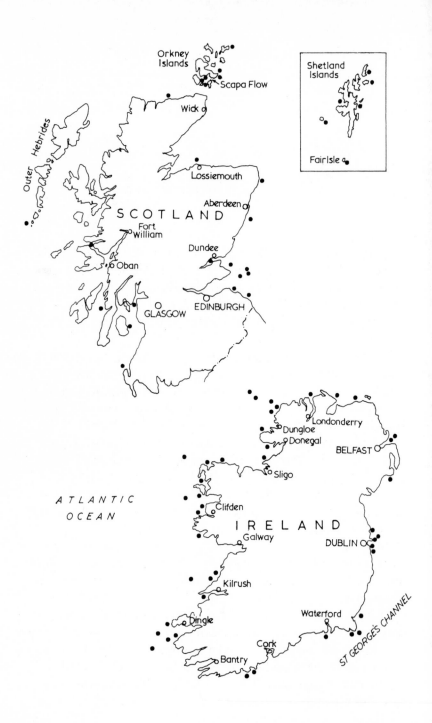

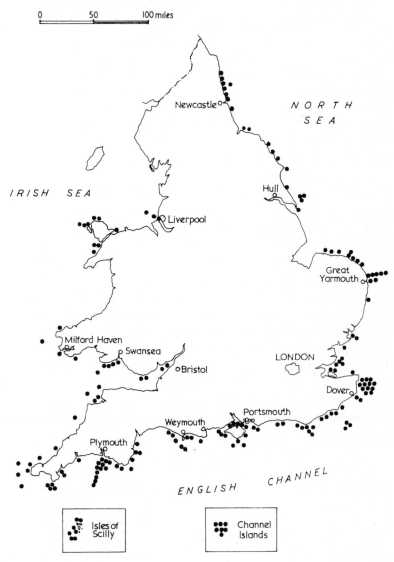

BLACK DOTS INDICATE APPROXIMATE
POSITION OF SHIPWRECKS DESCRIBED

0   50   100 miles

NORTH SEA

IRISH SEA

Newcastle

Hull

Liverpool

Great Yarmouth

Milford Haven

Swansea

Bristol

LONDON

Dover

Weymouth

Portsmouth

Plymouth

ENGLISH CHANNEL

Isles of Scilly

Channel Islands

to the nearest ten thousand. To credit each county that borders on the sea in this country with 2,000 shipwrecks would be no exaggeration, and in certain areas, particularly the south west, the Isle of Wight, the Goodwin Sands and the east coast, twice that number may have come to grief. It would therefore not be an unreasonable starting point to suggest that at a *minimum* some 250,000 wrecks have occurred.

In these islands, the disaster of shipwreck has been exploited to the full. But there is an even darker aspect of wreck, one that transcends the mere accidental loss of human life, and that is the ambivalence concerning personal and legal rights. In the Middle Ages, the Crown saw shipwreck as an opportunity to swell treasury funds at little or no expense to authority. Since the rewards were high, those appointed to look after the interests of the monarch were for the most part more concerned to fill their own pockets than to serve their master. The majority of counties suffered the appointment of an Admiral charged with ensuring that the Crown received its share of wreck, but more often than not these gentlemen were in direct competition with their lords, since both sides knew only too well that they were stealing. Possibly the greatest controversy in legal history has revolved around what is termed the 'right of wreck', since ownership of items of shipwreck has been the subject of countless Orders in Council, Proclamations, Acts of Parliament, High Court injunctions, writs, legal wrangles and prosecutions.

Undeniably, men have murdered their fellows for less than a shilling or a pair of boots; but when one has neither, such actions assume a different perspective. One must not overlook the gross social injustice and economic selfishness rampant in the seventeenth and eighteenth centuries. A labourer caught taking a pair of trousers from a shipwreck could be deported to the colonies for five years, whereas men such as Lord Zouch or the Duke of Buckingham thought nothing of extorting sums like £3,100 from the owner of a ship before restoring the owner's own cargo. This happened at Dover in the sixteenth century when the *Anne Lyon* came ashore. In stark contrast, when another merchantman was stranded on nearby Goodwin Sands a month later, it took the combined effort of every boatman in Ramsgate (of which there were some 300) a whole week to transfer her cargo, pump her out, and refloat the vessel. For their labours the men received £90 between them. No wonder survivors faced two ordeals if they were fortunate enough to reach land from a shipwreck: the sea itself, and the men on the beach—with every chance that the second would be far more cruel than the first.

This book is only a glimpse of the true picture, the turning of a page in history, and an attempt to put shipwreck into its rightful place, since it has been a subject sadly neglected. A great deal of our past lies on the seabed. Regardless of how it came to be there, these pages are a catalogue of appalling waste, not only of material but also human endeavour and lives. This continues to the present day, despite modern technology, legislation, and attempts to make ships more safe, for the sea has an insatiable appetite. Here in my own county of Cornwall, during the winter months when I started this book in 1977/8, six vessels were lost with twenty-eight dead. With the winter gales tearing the £1m trawler *Conqueror* to pieces in Mount's Bay, coastguards near Trevose Head were recovering corpses, so mangled by the sea as to make it impossible to tell whether they were from the Lowestoft trawler *Boston Sea Ranger*, the 500-ton coaster *Union Crystal*, the French *Gilles et Michel*, or the Danish coaster *Lady Kamilla*, all of which were total losses. While the manuscript was still only half completed there came the appalling news that the Fastnet race had claimed nineteen lives. Unsuspecting yachtsmen were hit by a full gale, and damaged and derelict craft were being towed into almost every west-country port. As 1979 drew to a close, and the last chapter was being typed, probably the worst gale of the century, gusting up to 170 mph, struck Devon and Cornwall, turning the sea into a maelstrom. The French trawler *Atria*, and two others simply vanished without trace; the 2,500-ton coaster *Skopelos Sky* became a total wreck near Port Isaac, on the north coast of Cornwall. In

Devon, the 420-ton coaster *Heye-P*, was wrecked at Prawle Point. Off the Lizard, the burnt-out and abandoned American tug *Gulf Majesty* drifted around for a week, whilst the 19,000-ton rig-construction barge she had been helping to tow, *Intermac-600*, was blown ashore under Gribben Head, a little over a mile from my cliff-top home. Unlike the majority of craft that go ashore in Cornwall, *Intermac-600* was saved, due solely to her unique construction, which was fortunate for her owners, J. Ray McDermott's, since she is the largest floating object ever to go ashore on this coast. Built at a cost approaching £20m, the gross weight of this 500ft-long barge, with her deck cargo of oil-rig components, cranes and machinery, was almost 40,000 tons. As the gales died away there came the sad news that the Scottish trawler *Bounteous*, had overturned at night in Mounts Bay, taking three of her crew to the bottom.

If therefore this book suggests a predominance of west-country shipwrecks, no apologies are necessary, since it is a matter of historical fact that Cornwall is *the* 'wreckers' county', and recent winters only serve to prove the point.

January 1981   *Richard Larn*
                                                         Carlyon Bay
                                                          Cornwall

I

THE RIGHT OF WRECK

1100–1599

During the early part of the twelfth century (when we have the earliest reference to shipwreck in the British Isles), and for several hundred years after, vessels cast ashore were considered of such little importance in themselves that their names were seldom if ever recorded. The sole interest of the authorities concerned only the 'Right of Wreck', with no regard for the ship itself, nor its crew. The fact that this legal expression has survived through the ages to this very day, and probably appears more often in State documents and papers than any other, demonstrates the great financial benefit and value placed on this most ancient and infamous privilege.

'Right of Wreck' refers to the legal beneficiary of shipwreck in a particular area, regardless of whether the item concerned be cargo, ship's stores, part of the fabric of a vessel, or a complete ship. Nine hundred years ago, when it was inconceivable that man would one day fly over the sea, or would use the oceans for recreation, then the expression 'wreck' was defined as simply a part or whole vessel or its contents, and in consequence the 'Right of Wreck' was an exceptionally lucrative and jealously guarded perquisite of the rich. In the twentieth century, the expression 'wreck' embraces not only ships and cargo but anything unnatural to the sea, including such things as crashed aircraft, dead animals, dinghies, sports equipment and the like, provided it is on or under the surface, within our territorial waters, or ashore below the highest spring tide mark.

Since these 'Rights' were often the subject of disputes and hence appeals as far back as 1114, it must be presumed that the practice was already long-established, possibly dating back to the Roman Conquest. Unlike national law, which is influenced by local customs and characteristics, maritime law deals with the usage of only two classes of people, merchants and mariners. Therefore maritime law differs but little between individual nations. The earliest identifiable sea code known to the western world, the Rolls of Oleron or Jugemens d'Oléron, was adopted successively by France, England and then Spain, having originated in the Mediterranean. Those responsible for drafting the Rolls of Oleron well appreciated the problems and injustices of 'wrecking', since they include a section which clearly specifies that ownership of a ship or cargo is not forfeit simply because accident brings it ashore:

> Ashyp, on entering into a haven or elsewhere, by chaunce breaketh yp and perysseth, and the mayster, maryners and merchaunts dye, theyr goodes are cast on the coast or remayne in the sea without any pursyte on the parte of those to whome they belonge, for they know nothynge, in siche a case, the whiche is very piteouse, the lord ought to set persons to save the sayd goodes, and these goodes the lord ought to guard and place safely and afterwards he ought to make known to the reletives or reletion of the dead drowned the misfortune and paye the sayd salvors after the labour and payne that they have taken, not at his own expense but at the expense of the thynges saved, and the resedue the which remayneth, the sayd lord ought to guard or have guarded entirely till a yere, unless those to whom the sayd goodes belonge come sooner. At the ende of a yere passed or more, if it pleaseth the sayd lord to wayte, he ought to sell publically and to the highest offerer the sayd thyngs, and from the money receved he ought to have prayer made to God for the dead, or to marrye poor maydes, or to do other workes after reason and consience. And he who shall do the contrarie and shall take any of the goodes of the sayd poor persons shypwrecked, lost and drwoned agaynst theyr desire and wyll, he is excominicated from the church, this is the judgment.

Fine words indeed, and a general principle which was to

The Needles Rocks and lighthouse, at the south-west corner of the Isle of Wight, showing the strong tides which sweep through the Needles Channel, and over the wreck sites of the *St Anthony*, *Campen*, *Assurance* and *Pomone* *(RLC)*

An early iron-banded cannon, mounted as a swivel gun, salvaged from the Spanish 'silver' wreck, near the Lizard, in 1976. The ship, lost in 1612, led to the first Lizard lighthouse. Apart from the great treasure recovered at the time, it has since yielded several hundred silver 'pieces of eight' *(RLC)*

Silver pieces of eight, or 8 Reales, of the type mentioned in this inventory of July 1628, when Jacob Johnson the 'dyver' salvaged 2360 'Ryalls of Eight Spanish Coyne' from the wreck of the Dutch East Indiaman *Campen*, lost near the Needles, Isle of Wight, during 1627 *(RLC)*

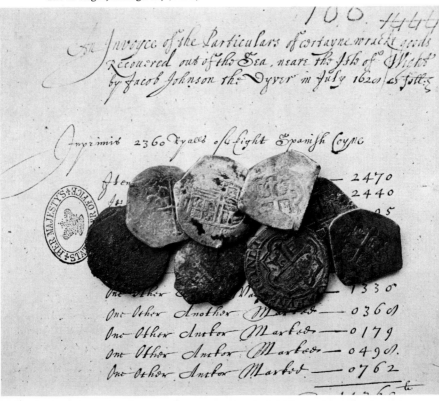

become the basis of our current Wreck Law, but as will be seen, our medieval ancestors thought more of their pockets and bellies than their souls.

Typical of Royal grants concerning the 'Right of Wreck' was that made by Henry I, in the early 1100s, to the Abbot of Tavistock in Devon. This allowed him and the church 'all the Churches of Sully (Isles of Scilly) and the appurtenances, also all the wrecks except for whale and a whole ship'. These exceptions were not unusual, and more often than not included porpoise, dolphin, sturgeon, ambergris, even puffins. All these were of considerable value, both as food or a source of raw material; an intact ship could be armed and incorporated into the King's fleet as a man o'war.

To what extent shipping plied the waters around the British Isles at this time is uncertain. Few vessels would have exceeded 100 tons, and since hardly any ventured further than the Mediterranean, the overall volume of sea traffic must be presumed small, with the bulk limited to coastal traffic working between England, France, the Lowlands and Ireland. The towns of Dover, Sandwich and Romney, later joined by Hastings and Hythe made up the famous Cinque Ports, from whence communications were maintained with our territory across the Channel. For this reason, the area between mainland Kent and the Goodwin Sands (known as the Downs) became a most important anchorage, where ships awaited a fair wind to proceed into the North Sea or down Channel, or to form a convoy, and the volume of shipwreck as a consequence can be measured by the number of disputes concerning wrecks or wreck goods. In Norfolk, near Blakeney, a ship laden with cloth and other merchandise to the value of £14,000 went ashore during a storm in February 1282. The owners, Henry Flik and Helebrand de Lubek, merchants of Alman, complained to the king that they had left the wreck in fear of death, so brutal was the treatment given them by locals who carried off the goods. Similar treatment was received by the crew of a vessel wrecked at Dengemareys (Dengemarsh), within the fee of the Abbot of Battle in

February 1286, in fact the wreckers killed Vincent Estefne, a merchant on board, before making off with the cargo. Within the Downs, a William Martyn, described as a shipowner, was unfortunate enough to lose a vessel near Sandwich. His appeal to the crown dated 7 June 1298, states that whilst returning from Flanders with armour and other goods, his ship was cast away and plundered of its cargo. He requested a jury be appointed to investigate his claim, in order that his property could be restored, but no action resulted. In another example, thirteen years later, the Lord of the Manor of Hummanby, a village near Filey Brigg, Yorkshire, is brought to our attention over a case of so called 'plunder'. The 'Right of Wreck' here had been vested in the manor since 1066, and had never belonged to the Crown. None the less, the King himself ordered an inquiry to establish what Richard de Lacy had done with 'a chest of gold florentines and silver coins to the value of £300, and silver in bar to a greater sum, cast ashore at Fyley, which as wreck of the sea belongs to his Majesty'. The outcome remains unrecorded but in 1318, only seven years after, another ship was wrecked at the same place. In this instance the only value lay in the vessel's masts and tackle, which after salvage was valued at only 40 shillings. Not surprisingly, the Crown conveniently ignored the previous dispute, the sum being trivial, and de Lacy received the full amount without question. In all these and many similar reports, few make reference to the identity of the ships lost, and it was 1348 before we hear that the *Katherine* was wrecked at Flamborough:

> Evil-doers broke into the ship and the chests were carried away; 200 florins belonging to the king, and 100 marks of the money to the mariners.

The protesting voice of Robert Constable, the local lord of the manor, was still ringing in the courts, when the king ordered his arrest on charges of piracy on the high seas!

Between 1340 and 1357 the first of the Admiralty Courts sat to deal with the enforcement of maritime law. As a result, two or three local Admirals were appointed, namely of the 'north', and the 'south and west', who were charged with the administration of maritime affairs and incidents including shipwreck, in their respective areas. Amongst their duties they were to ensure that the Crown's royal share was collected in respect of everything washed ashore, and as an inducement the Admirals were allowed to retain a small percentage. This system encouraged gross irregularities, and in consequence the Admirals grew fat and rich on their 'privilege', namely the proceeds of shipwrecks of which the Crown was never informed. On stretches of the coast where the 'Right of Wreck' was held by one of the gentry and not the Crown, disputes frequently arose concerning boundaries where these 'rights' began and ended, not only in respect to the foreshore but offshore, since floating wreckage recovered by boats at sea was equally lucrative. Our twentieth-century disputes concerning territorial fishing rights are in principle similar to the problems concerning sovereignty of the sea which existed over 500 years ago, except that then the claims were to dominion over whole oceans. In the fifteenth century, Pope Alexander declared:

> By the Authority of Almighty God, having drawn a line on the known globe north and south, dividing the Atlantic in two; that everything to the west shall belong to Spain, everything to the east undiscovered or not, shall belong to Portugal.

The line to which the Pope referred was at first drawn 100 leagues west of the Cape Verde Islands, but following complaints from the King of Portugal that this gave his ships insufficient sea-room when en route for the Cape of Good Hope, the distance was extended to 270 leagues, or midway between the Azores and the West Indies. Such claims were finally overturned in the seventeenth century, in what has become aptly described as the 'Battle of the Books'. Around the British Isles, the extent of its territorial waters and the offshore limits of the 'Right of Wreck' have been estimated variously and by strange standards. Bartolus of Saxo Ferrato (a celebrated legal light of the fourteenth century) stated that 'the jurisdiction of the sea extended for 100 miles from any coast'. At other times the distance has been judged to be 'as far as an arrow may fly', or 'as far as a cannon shot', even 'as far as a man can see seaward'. In Devon, the Courtnay family claimed wreck 'as far out to sea as a man on horseback can see an umber barrel'; in Yorkshire it was 'as far as a man can ride into the sea and stick a spear in the bottom', and at Beachy Head, Sussex, 'as far as a man can reach on horseback at low water'. But these and variations were so obviously open to misinterpretation as to be useless, and in practice possession was nine-tenths of the law.

Not surprisingly, wreck incidents associated with the Cinque Ports are the best-documented for the period, since their administrator, the Lord Warden, appears to have been in an almost permanent dispute with the Lord High Admiral of England and the Narrow Seas (the Straits of Dover), with members of the royal court and with Lords of the Manors over the 'Right of Wreck'. A local landowner, in a letter addressed to Henry VIII dated 22 January 1533, wrote:

> Twelve ships have been lost this winter on the Goodwin Sands with divers merchandise, and when men of the port of Dover have gone out for their safeguard the servants of the Lord Warden have taken from them their findalls, contrary to their liberties. Certain kyntletts were found by divers persons and were taken from them, and only a crown was given them as a reward, although some of the kyntletts were full of wine and gold, and they are supposed to be treasure ships. All this has been witheld from the owners. When men have been found on the sea sand, their garments and their purses have been taken from them and their bodies left unburied and eaten by hogs and dogs.

Of all our sixteenth-century shipwrecks, including those of the Spanish Armada, none have become better known than the *Mary Rose*, which foundered on 19 July 1545, with the loss of men variously quoted as between 400 and 700. Seldom has any shipwreck been witnessed by such an august assembly as that gathered near Southsea Castle, Portsmouth, that day.

The French were actively threatening invasion of the Isle of Wight, and the impending battle brought the King and his entire court to Southsea, where a great army was already encamped. The fleet was just leaving Portsmouth harbour, in readiness to engage the enemy, which was creeping round the eastern end of the Wight. The *Great Harry* was in the van, followed by the *Mary Rose*, leading a great line of men o' war into battle. It is doubtful whether the *Mary Rose* fired as much as a single broadside before a combination of mis-handling unstable design, and open gunports too close to the waterline, combined to allow the sea to flood the hold, and she sank. The topmasts of the wreck were left protruding above the surface, and some twenty-five to thirty men saved their lives by clinging to them. But there was no hope for those between decks, or the officers and troops clad in heavy armour.

Within two weeks of her loss, pontoons were positioned over the wreck, and sixty English seamen assisted by thirty-one Venetians were engaged in passing cables beneath the hull for a tidal lift. It appears that nothing went right for them, and by 5 August the demands on the time and resources of the Royal Dockyard were so intolerable that the Superinten-dent wrote in a letter:

> So charged all the kynges Majesties shypwrychts with makying engyns for the same that they have no leisure to attend any other thyng.

The Lord Admiral, Vincent Lisle, reported to the Duke of Suffolk that same day, that the wreck would be up by the afternoon, or the next day at the latest. But the next day came and went, the summer slipped away, and still the *Mary Rose* remained on the seabed. Priority then moved from the re-covery of the vessel to the salvage of her guns and fittings. This continued for about four years, after which the incident faded into obscurity, and the wreck remained undisturbed until 16 June 1836. At that time, the brothers John and Charles Deane, who were responsible for the basic invention of the rigid or standard diving helmet apparatus, were employed in the Solent to demolish the wreck of the *Royal George*, which capsized and sank in 1782. While engaged in this work, the divers were approached by some local fishermen to recover some nets, foul of some obstruction on the bottom, nearer to Southsea Castle. This obstruction turned out to be the timbers of an old wreck, and the recovery of a 12ft bronze cannon, weighing over two and a half tons, proved it to be the *Mary Rose*. Over the following weeks several more guns were salvaged, and numerous artefacts including longbows, arrows, armour and stone shot, after which the site was abandoned for the second time. For 131 years it lay undisturbed, until 1967, when as part of a project initiated by Alexander McKee, a local historian, author and amateur diver, the site was again re-located, and eventual excavation suggested that at least half of the hull remained intact in the deep mud. Work is currently in progress excavating the vessel, after which it is planned that it will be salvaged intact, floated on a pontoon into a permanent museum in Portsmouth, to become a unique display item of Tudor craftsmanship.

Apart from some early broadsheets, the richest source of material concerning shipwrecks of this period is the Calendars of Domestic State Papers (SP.Dom), although much of the correspondence on the subject is unfortunately brief and often lacking in detail. From such documents we read that on 5 April 1547 the Lord Proctor Somerset was informed of the *Clement* of London, carrying eight lasts of superfine gunpowder and other war stores belonging to the King, which had been lost near Newcastle. From the meagre evidence available, it appears that Captain Wilson mistook a church steeple 5 miles from Tynemouth for some other mark, and put his ship ashore. In Norfolk, a Scottish vessel was wrecked at Runton in 1577, which resulted in a petition to the King's Council, Sir Edward Clese having claimed the entire cargo for himself. Meanwhile on the Goodwin Sands various unnamed wrecks took place during 1542/3, at least three in 1544, several more between 1550 and 1580, and the *Dolphin* in 1585. But the greatest shipwreck tragedy of the century was about to happen with the loss of more than one third of the Spanish Armada of 1588.

From the day of its conception, 'La Armada Felicissima' or, 'The Most Fortunate Fleet of His Catholic Majesty Phillip II', was doomed to failure. It was doomed because the entire enterprise was too long in preparation, and because its architect assumed total mastery of the sea. More important, it relied on an army and an equally massive fleet to arrive at a rendezvous, without hindrance from the enemy or weather, although fleet and army were several hundred miles apart. Its appointed leader, Medina Sidonia, was no seaman; he had never once commanded a ship, let alone a fleet, and his inadequacy caused him to plead more than once to be relieved of this responsibility. On 28 May 1588, a total of 138 ships left Lisbon, carrying over 30,000 men, two-thirds of whom were never to see Spain again. The outcome of the venture was a complete disaster, and a catalogue of wreck on an unprecedented scale, which left Spanish ships strewn down the length of the western shores of Scotland and Ireland, from Fair Isle to Bantry Bay. Only one minor straggler was lost on English soil, this being the *San Pedro Mayor*, a hospital ship wrecked in Bigbury Bay, Devon. Harassed by the English fleet in the Channel, then scattered by fireships off Gravelines, where several were stranded, the remainder of the great Armada fled northwards, intent on rounding Scotland and returning to Lisbon by way of the Irish coast and the Bay of Biscay. At least twenty-five ships are known to have sunk around the British Isles. In Scotland, the *Gran Griffon* and the vessel popularly known as the 'Tobermory galleon' were the first victims. The former anchored off Fair Isle, between Orkney and Shetland, on 27 September, but sank close inshore the following day. The cause of her loss is uncertain, but no doubt she was leaking as a result of storm and battle, and with a much dejected crew, physically exhausted after days at the pumps—they probably simply gave up the fight.

The remains of the ship have since been relocated in Stroms Hellier, a narrow inlet under towering cliffs. The social impact of some 300 unwelcome enemy seamen, thrust upon such a lonely community, themselves ill-provisioned for winter, can be well imagined. When finally their enforced stay ended in mid-November, fifty of their number were left behind, having died of hunger.

The Tobermory galleon has always been something of a mystery, since whilst the existence of the actual wreck is well established, its identity remains unsolved, and the truth as to the supposed treasure on board will probably never be known. The circumstances leading up to the wreck are not in question. She arrived in Tobermory seeking shelter and fresh food and water, and while out foraging for supplies, the Spaniards captured Donald M'Lean, and kept him as a hostage. In an act of revenge and self-destruction, M'Lean fired the ship's magazine, killing some 500 of the enemy. There are four names popularly given to the ship, the *Florentina*, *Florentine*, *San Juan Bautista*, of Sicily, and *San Juan de Sicilia*, but which is correct remains uncertain. Repeated salvage attempts have been made since 1655, when Archibald Miller of Greenock, and others, were the first to use a diving bell on the wreck. Miller was most successful in the salvage of guns and other valuable items, but no treasure was found. It is the evidence of a single sentence in his report which has caused later generations to believe the vessel carried treasure. No other record exists to support the theory, and the degree of success, or rather the lack of success, achieved by the many salvage operations over the years, substantiates the theory that the Tobermory galleon was never a treasure ship. In all aspects, Miller's report is utterly convincing, and his phraseology is exactly what one would expect of a diver, so one is inclined to believe him. Whether or not that all-important sentence is true is for the reader to decide:

Information by Archibald Miller, about the ship sunk in Tobermory, in the Sound of Mull, the ships name is the *Fflorence*, of Spain.

26

The ship lies sunk off the shore, about one finger stone cast, her stern lies unto the shore northwest, and her head to the southwest. She lies under the water at the deepest nine fathom at a low water, and twelve fathom at a full sea or high-water. There is no deck upon her except in the hinder part. There is a great heap of timber which I take to be the cabin. I did see one door there which I take to be the steerage door, and within that door I did see a number of dishes both great and small of a white bluish colour, but whether they are pewter or plate (silver) I know not.

Near this place I did see one great gun and her muzzle up right on end, as big or bigger than the gun I lifted which would carry a 48lb ball. There is a great heap of cannon shot about midships and upon the shot lies three iron guns. In the forepart of the ship lies many great ballast stones and some shot amongst them, and there we found one silver bell, about 4cwt. We got within the ship at a pretty distance, the first great gun with two other, all being brass guns, the great gun is eleven feet length and seven inches and one fourth part of measure in the bore. The other two were minions. We also got two demy culverins, two falcons, two slings, all brass.

We lifted three anchors whereof one was eighteen foot in length, the other was fifteen and the thing was iron. I got two brass sheaves weighing sixty pounds, I lifted also the rudder, and took eight iron pykes of it. It was twenty-eight foot in length, but there was one piece broken off the same. I lifted the capstan of curious work, pawled with a spring at every inches end, I cannot tell the bigness, the thing I found would have been two feet in the diameter.

I saw something like a coat of arms, but I could not reach it being entangled. I saw gilt upon several standing pieces of the ship. *I saw one paper of Latin extracted out of the Spanish records, that there were thirty millions of cash on board the said ship, and it tells it lay under the sill of the gunroom.*

The lieutenant of the ship reports the same to the Earl of Argyle, I mean the Marques's father, and which paper holds good by the lieutenants report. I found something like metal between the ship and shore in soft ooze ground in several places, and think they are guns. The properest time to dive is to begin about the 20th of May and continue until the midst of August. I found a crown or diadem and had hooked same, but being chained it fell amongst the timbers. This crown is also in the Spanish records. I think the goods of the ship may be recovered provided the timber could be carried away, and I do not doubt that it may be taken away, provided my pains and expenses be allowed and to show that this is not a simulat information, though I be an old man, I am willing yet to go alone upon due consideration for it is a pity that such a great business should be lost where it may be by industry.

As witness my hand at Greenock this twentieth day of November 1683. I was master of the whole employment, myself for the spare diver.

Archibald Miller

Ownership of the wreck was vested in the Argyle family from the day the ship sank, and the Dukes have sponsored and encouraged several salvage operations. Between World Wars I and II a number of pewter plates, a few silver coins, carpenters' tools and iron shot were recovered, but little of any significant value. In the 1950s, when the last serious salvage operation took place, the legendary 'Buster' Crabbe found a religious medallion, which was lost by accident over the side of the salvage boat.

The value of any contents of other Armada wrecks is now more attractive than ever before, although the majority were probably worked during the seventeenth and eighteenth centuries. In Ulster the great galleons *Girona* and the *Trinidad Valencera* have both been found in recent years. From the former has come a collection of almost priceless jewellery, now on permanent display in the Belfast City Museum. Four hundred years earlier Sir George Carew reported in a letter, written at Dunmore Castle, County Clare:

Already we have salvaged three pieces of artillery of brass. Yesterday we fastened our hawsers to a cannon of battery or basalyke, as we supposed by the length, for they lie at four fathom and a half of water, which was so huge that it break our cables. Our diver was nearly drowned, but Irish *aqua vitae* hath such virtues as I hope for his recovery. If the diver of Dublin were here with his instruments I would not doubt to bring good store of artillery from hence; for if I be not deceived out of our boat we did plainly see four pieces more.

In Blacksod Bay, County Mayo, the locals plundered the

Genoese carrack *La Rata Encordnada* as she lay stranded and on fire in the shallows, whilst the people of Dunbeg and Troma, County Clare, stripped two more. West Donegal was the scene of at least one Spanish loss, since bronze cannon, lead ingots and coin have all been found off Gola Island. Other known sites include the *Duquesa Santa Anna* in Loughros Mor Bay; *San Juan* and the *Lavia*, along with four others in Donegal Bay; two near Broadhaven, *El Gran Grin* on Clare Island and the *Falcon Blanco Mediano* on Inishbaffin Island. There are at least eight others between Galway Bay and Cape Clear.

The latter part of 1592 saw great excitement in south-east Kent, and at Deal and Ramsgate in particular, following the wreck of three large and very valuable ships on the Goodwin Sands. Already notorious for shipwrecks, it is doubtful if this area has ever seen such wealth before or since, despite the thousand or so vessels lost there. Endless squabbles ensued over the 'Right of Wreck', and the value of the cargoes can be gauged from the fact that judicial proceedings were still in progress three years later. Two of the ships were Dutch, the *St Peter* of Amsterdam, and the *Golden Lion* of Middleburg. The third was English, a London-owned vessel named *Red Lion*.

Local boatmen were the first on the scene after the *St Peter* stranded sometime between 15 and 23 November, and proceeded to make every use of five whole days of calm weather to pursue the age-old custom of 'wrecking', and to strip the vessel before the great 'ship swallower' engulfed the hull. Acting on direct orders from the King, Lord Cobham convened a court at which several boat owners were questioned under oath as to their accomplices during visits to the wreck, who actually went aboard and what was recovered. The original depositions survive, and resentment of authority and suspicion is evident in every statement recorded. One man made sure that everyone in his boat was implicated, having given a small share of a bale of cloth to each, and what better way to enlist the sympathy of the local parson than by making sure that 'he accepted three or four razors, a pair or two of kynves, and a dozen spectacles or more'!

Court proceedings were still in full swing when the second wreck occurred, followed in December by the *Red Lion*. Any possible legal actions were now quite impossible, otherwise the entire population of every coastal village and town in Kent would have been summoned. A token prosecution was served on Richard Bassett of Ramsgate, who admitted taking several sowes of lead from the *Golden Lion*, each of 300lbs, which he had sold to John Duck, of Rye, for 23s 10d. Unfortunately, history does not record what punishment or fine was imposed.

2

THE ROAD TO THE EAST

1600–1699

Although the total of Dutch East Indiamen wrecked around the British Isles during the seventeenth century probably numbered no more than ten ships, their very size and richness brought about an era of salvage, which saw the introduction of commercial diving in this country. The value of these ships was such that they were the target of professional salvors, especially if one 'fell to land' on a stretch of coast remote from authority, or if there was no clear-cut ownership of wrecked goods. The early 1600s saw the consolidation of the Dutch East India Company or United Netherlands Chartered East India Company (VOC), which began with four ships sailing for the East in 1594, quickly followed by its English equivalent, more commonly known as the 'John Company'. In time similar companies sprang up in France, Denmark and Sweden, but it was the Dutch and English which rose to become the most powerful trading organisations the world has ever known. Vasco da Gama unlocked the door to the East when, in 1497, he made the first European sea passage to India and thus established Portuguese supremacy over a vast area, upsetting all cosmogony and accepted customs of trading.

Until then, most trade external to Europe was overland, using caravans across the heart of Asia, or else by way of the Red Sea and Persian Gulf. By these routes, priceless commodities such as pepper, nutmeg, cloves, cinnamon, ginger, damask, silk, porcelain, rubies, pearls, sandalwood and dyewood reached the western world. From Japan, China, India and the Spice Islands such luxuries were stacked high in Levantine port warehouses, awaiting shipment to Venice and Genoa, and from there to the rest of Europe. At least that was the situation until 1595, when the Dutch, attracted by vast profits, challenged the Portuguese, having discovered the 'secret' route. Unlike the Dutch, whose first adventure in the East was profitable in a business sense, the initial English expedition was nothing short of disastrous, since (in complete ignorance of the market) London merchants sent out heavy woollen garments, serge trousers and leather boots. Totally unacceptable in a tropical climate, the clothing was useless; and instead of appreciation for English iron cooking-pots and platters, the natives were eating from china and porcelain dishes, the like of which the English merchants had never before seen. Outward bound, these Indiamen carried silver specie, with which to purchase their return cargo. Homeward, they were loaded to the gunwhales with every conceivable valuable, often to the point that the ship's armament, vital in case of attack by pirates, was struck down into the hold in order to make more cargo space.

A wrecked ship in this category was therefore of immense value, possibly worth two or three million pounds by today's standards. Consequently, along with more conventional shipping disasters, the squabbles over ownership and 'right' persisted, becoming more complex as the value increased, and because the Dutch government was not easily dissuaded from relinquishing its property. An example which forceably illustrates the point is the case investigated by the Admiralty Court at Dover Castle on 10 August 1602. Presided over by Lord Cobham, depositions and statements were taken concerning the events of a 'wreck of canvas' at Hope, near Cliff's End, Thanet, of *thirty years before* as well as details of a ship carrying deals, copper, wax and other valuables lost *eighteen to twenty years before*. The Lord Warden's enjoyment of wreck was under challenge by a John Henderson, Lord of the Manor of Folkestone, who used the following facts to support his case:

The Manor of Folkstone was in the hands of Lord Clinton and Baron Say (Sir James Fiennes), and afterwards of Henry VIII. Edward VI granted it to Edward Lord Clinton, who surrendered it to Queen Mary. She granted it to Lord Clinton and Say as a deed recited, and by divers conveyances it is now vested in Henderson. By extents of the said Manor (35 & 47 year of reign of Henry III) it seems that the right of wreck belongs to the Manor, as also by quo warranto 2 & 7 Edward I and 6 Edward II. The question is, whether the wrecks of the sea happening on the sands or the seashore adjoining the town or Manor of Folkstone, belong to the Lord Warden, or John Henderson?

In passing, the time scale of the argument is most interesting since the case was heard in 1602 (Queen Elizabeth), and the defendant was freely quoting precedents and titles of 1251 (Henry III), 1274 (Edward I) and 1313 (Edward II)! At the time of the latter of the two shipwrecks in question, a Thomas Paramore of Minster, servant to Sir Edward Wotton, went on board the vessel. But, realising that he had come only to spy for his master, 'the Ramsgate men then aboard had beaten and tumbled him overboard, and had broken three or four of his men's heads'—whereupon Sir Edward bade him demand soilage and groundage of the ship instead, since he had no 'right' to wreck. No doubt the same level of argument was in progress in Norfolk, where an Edinburgh-owned vessel (William Brown Master), was wrecked near Yarmouth on 28 May 1607, while carrying hides, cloth and £5,000–£6,000 sterling.

The first Dutch East Indiaman wreck extant in the 1600s was a ship stranded at Burling-gate, in the Parish of East Dean, beyond Beachy Head, Sussex, at the end of April 1617. Unnamed, she was described by eyewitnesses as 'richly laden with bullion, specie etc', and was promptly claimed by a Mr Payne, who held the Manor on lease. The Dutch factor, James Sutton, applied to the Admiralty Court for restitution of the cargo, but was told that Lord Zouch, Warden of the Cinque Ports, would deal with the matter.

The number of ships lost around the British Isles was

already beginning to escalate, a steady increase which continued well into the nineteenth century, and reached a peak in the 1860s when three ships a day were being wrecked. Following the East Indiaman in 1617, the *John* of Southampton was lost near Hythe in December of that year, for which the Lord Warden placed a bond of £200 on Robert Hudson, Hume Ambler and Roger Dye, all haberdashers of London, as indemnity for the return of their goods, presumably cargo carried on board. The year after, 1618, the *Golden Wagon* was wrecked near Dover and may well have been a Dutch vessel, since she originated from Emden, in East Friesland; also the *Blind Fortune*, the *Sampson* and the *Ark Noah*, the latter carrying cinnamon, pepper and specie, of which forty casks, four bags and the equivalent of £4,000 respectively were saved.

But all these were overshadowed by the *Anne Lyon*. This incident took place in November 1623, when coin to the value of £9,000 was taken from the wreck near Sandwich and locked up in Deal Castle. Inhabitants of the coastal towns and villages blatantly looted the ship, and although the authorities looked to Sir Henry Mainwaring to restore order, he was more concerned to get to the castle. There he tried to persuade the sergeant-at-arms to slit open the bags of specie (which probably bore certain marks of ownership), so that when the merchants arrived, they would be unable to identify individual property. On this occasion Lord Zouch received £1,100 merely for returning some Brazil wood, a hard reddish wood of the East Indian sappan tree, to its rightful owners, and a further £2,000 for sugar, spice, and other items.

This continuous loss of valuable Dutch vessels in particular, at least twelve in five years, caused the Dutch government to suggest that the Goodwin Sands should be marked with a light or beacon. With justification, the English claimed that since the Dutch has lost the most ships and most wanted the beacon, they should contribute the most money, a suggestion that was not well received in Amsterdam. Caution was in fact rewarded, not because the English erected a

The traditional location of the temporary grave of Sir Cloudesley Shovel at Porth Hellick, Isles of Scilly, following his death by drowning after his ship, HMS *Association*, was wrecked on October 1707 *(F.E. Gibson)*

A late 16th-century bronze swivel gun, salvaged from 90ft of water near Padstow, Cornwall. Local tradition, that a Spanish vessel sank on a deep-water reef known as Galleon Rock, proved to be correct *(RLC)*

Captain Lydiard RN, of
HM Frigate *Anson*, who lost his life in
the wreck of 1807 attempting to save the
life of a young boy *(J. Gold, engraving)*

A wreck poster of 1812, advertising
shipwrecked goods for sale, salvaged
from the galliot *Maria*, lost on Tresco
(RLC)

For Sale by Auction

WRECK

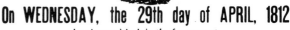

On WEDNESDAY, the 29th day of APRIL, 1812
by eleven o'clock in the forenoon at

ST. MARYS, ISLES OF SCILLY

the following goods partly damaged and subject to such conditions as
shall then and there be produced

3668 Bundles of iron rod	1424 Cast iron pots
63 Iron boilers	11 Iron tea kettles
13 Boxes of tinned plate	160 Sheets tinplate
166 Kegs of round shot	5 Cases of sheet iron
179 Firkins of butter	1 Cask of cudbear
10 Pipes of linseed oil	4 Casks of white lead
2 Cases of English China	47 Dozen files
592 Pieces of woolen cloth	2 Cases, 1 box of hats
550 Pieces of long cloth	80 Pieces barbozettes
24 Pieces of waistcoating	170 Pieces of bindings
449 Bundles and 507 skeins	86 Pieces Manchester Velvet
of cotton yard	3375 Spills cotton yarn
2 Cavalry saddles	23 Matted parcels
1 Case with writing desk	1 Case of cabbage seed

Subject to repayment of drawback and bounty of Excise and Customs
1012 pieces of printed calicoes, and for exportation 16 bags and a
quantity of loose coffee. Being part of the general cargo salved from
the wreck of the galiot "Maria". Thomas Jones Master, lost on Tresco
Island on her voyage from Liverpool to Oporto. A deposit of 33 per
cent is to be paid at time of sale and the remainder on delivery in Bank
of England notes. For viewing, catalogues or particulars apply four
days previous to Woolcock and Edwards, St. Marys.

BY ORDER
this 28th day of March, 1812

beacon themselves, but because of the fearful gale of 3/4 October 1624, which would most certainly have destroyed any such structure. A contemporary account of the storm described it as 'the most terrible gale, the like of which was never seen'; it sank twenty vessels in the Downs and put dozens of the 120 at anchor ashore on the sands and flats around Deal and Ramsgate. Two large vessels were also lost: a Dunkirker which exploded, killing 200 of her crew, and a Dutch ship. Both these gave ample employment to a newcomer on the scene, a man who earned his living by working underwater, a diver in fact, and the first to be mentioned as such in the State Papers of this country. Jacob Johnson, whose name was an Anglicised version of the Dutch, had probably been sent over by the East India Company Committee to recover some of its property. Little is known of the man, except that he owned a salvage craft named *Charity*, registered at Sandwich, lived in Kent, and quickly became an associate of the Duke of Buckingham, who later acted as his sponsor. In 1625 there was more work for 'the diver', when as part of a fleet of five English Indiamen, the *Moon* was lost near Dover on or about 25 September. The Duke sent Johnson to work the wreck, but warned others, 'Do not trust him, he thinks more of his belly and his back' (ie food and sleep).

Despite so many losses on this part of the south coast between Chichester and the Thames, it was still felt necessary to protect the interests that the Lord Warden of the Cinque Ports enjoyed. On 2 March, at Dover Castle, Sir George Newman stated that he could produce records to prove that all goods taken within 100 miles of the shore belonged to the Warden! No wonder the gentlemen pursued their share of wreck with such diligence. In a letter dated 8 March 1625, Sir John Hippisley wrote to Buckingham, 'The former bill of lading of the Hamburger was for a wrong vessel. This one lies at Deal, and can be got to shore for £100 and payment to the salvors, and is worth £100,000'.

If it appears that ships were being lost only in the vicinity of the Downs and Kent, it should be remembered that the bulk of shipping passed through the Straits of Dover (or the 'Narrow Sea' as it was then known), and in consequence this was the setting for countless incidents. Vessels lost elsewhere were often recorded only if of some particular importance, such as the report from Chester on 4 April 1625 that five transports from Liverpool bound for Carrickfergus had miscarried and were lost on Anglesey, with only 194 survivors from 500 troops aboard. The Mayor of Liverpool, on whom fell the responsibility and expense of feeding and clothing them, complained to the Council that 'unless the king compassionates the town, it will be the utter overthrow of that poor Corporation'. During the same year, wrecks reported included three ships at Barmston, south of Bridlington in East Yorkshire, one of which was a Dunkirk man o' war; an English ship run ashore near Aldborough; and a vessel sunk in the Cattewater, Plymouth.

1627 saw an extraordinary number of incidents, at places as far apart as Swansea and Corton, Appledore and Tynemouth, Scotland and Brunsey Castle, Hampshire. From the *Bristol* wreck, near St Marys, a chain of gold and £500 in coin were salvaged; since it was a prize vessel of Captain Ellis, the Council decreed that he be examined, to ascertain what else of value may have been aboard; while at Margate, in Kent, Sir John Hippisley, no doubt short of funds and unable to extract any other financial advantage from the *Anne*, of Woodbridge, stranded on the beach, took away her best anchor and cable 'as a fee for the ship's casting away'.

But the real money was to be found on the Needles, on the Isle of Wight. It was here, on 17 October, that three Dutch East Indiamen, outward bound for Batavia with rich cargoes and specie, with a large number of women and children passengers aboard, got off course in bad weather, and were wrecked on the south side of the Needles rocks. Part of a convoy, the wrecks included the *Campen* and *Flying Dragon*. But only the former carried the usual consignment of silver coin, that from the *Flying Dragon* having been transferred to another vessel. No sooner had news of the wrecks reached the Duke of Buckingham than he instructed Jacob the diver to proceed to the island, and salvage all he could. Amongst the State Papers held in the Public Records Office in London are a great many documents relating to these vessels, including a detailed account of items Johnson recovered. These included 15,562lbs of wrought and cast iron cannons and anchors, several hundred pigs of lead, weighing about 120lbs each, and 2,360 pieces of eight, or Mexican 'cobs', aptly described as 'Spanish Coyne'. The much-sought-after wreck of the *Campen* defied a number of twentieth-century attempts at relocation, which were thwarted by the almost total lack of underwater visibility in the Needles tide race, which can exceed four knots. Its rediscovery was by accident in 1979, when amateur divers from a Northampton club stumbled on the site. It is quite remarkable that about one hundred lead ingots, concentrated into one huge pile, and a very large quantity of silver coin, could survive in 25/30ft of water undiscovered for so long, especially since two groups of other divers have worked on the remains of HM man o' war *Assurance* (1753) for over eight years, on Goose Rock, less than 500 yards away.

Encouraged by the success of the Isle of Wight venture, Captain John Mason and Jacob Johnson applied to the Duke for authority to employ their skill elsewhere—on the great silver ship from St Lucar in particular, wrecked 'at the Lizard' in 1617. Carrying a vast quantity of silver in bars and coin, Sir John Killigrew recovered some of the cargo for himself, then threatened death to 'all persons who attempt to seek after the remainder'. He then used the wreck incident as a strong argument in support of his petition, to erect and maintain a light or beacon at the Lizard, to prevent other wrecks. Assumed for centuries to have been lost actually on the Lizard headland, the actual wreck site was relocated by accident in 1975 within a few hundred yards of Rill Head, but certainly still sufficiently close to the Lizard to be reckoned part of that area. The site has already yielded hundreds of silver 'cobs', or pieces of eight, an early 'built up' iron cannon (now in Southsea Castle Museum), sounding leads, and other artefacts of the period. Unfortunately for the salvors, the movement of seabed sand which uncovered the wreck has since worked against them, and the wreck now lies buried again.

Finding his attempts to dive at the Lizard frustrated by Killigrew, Jacob Johnson tried his hand on a wreck site immediately outside the entrance to Dartmouth harbour, on the eastern side. During 1629 he raised five pieces of ordnance from the ship, whereupon the mayor and the town clerk ordered him to cease salvage work unless he was prepared to share the proceeds with the town. Once more he found himself unable to follow his profession, owing mainly to the petty jealousy of minor officials. For one thing, these men resented his close working relationship with members of Court, despite the fact he was really no more than a skilled labourer. He spent seven months in attendance with the fleet at the Isle of Rhē in his hoy *Charity*, with 'no other allowance than that of an ordinary mariner', followed by a period of some five or six weeks as a prisoner of some Dunkirkers. On 6 March 1628, these had captured him along with his new 30-ton pink and five crew between Margate and Ramsgate. Johnson's financial plight was obviously desperate. The Duke owed him a considerable sum of money for his part in the ill-fated expedition, since in the diver's own words, 'Having performed service so extraordinary . . . you thought it fit to be rewarded'. If Buckingham saw fit not to reimburse Johnson on this occasion, there was no shortage of work for his special skills, since the Isle of Rhē fleet on its return to England was caught in Plymouth during a severe gale on 26 November 1627. By morning, fifteen ships were ashore in the Hamoaze, and five others in the Cattewater. Johnson was also busy at Castlehaven, Co Cork, in Eire, during the summer of 1630. A Spanish galleon captured by a vessel of the West India Company of the United Provinces of Holland was wrecked in the shallows on the western side of the entrance to the haven in December 1628. Since the Dutch West India Company had been granted free passage for all its ships by an Order in Council dated 5 September 1628, as well as the right to all wreck of their vessels cast away in His Majesty's Dominions, they were naturally incensed when the diver arrived—the more so since he not only dived on the wreck and removed various items, but lifted things which owner's workmen had freed and strapped ready for salvage! The Dutch petitioned Charles I to restrain Johnson from interfering again, and received royal approval, but the diver was too close to Buckingham and hence to the Crown for this to have any real restrictions on his activities.

The next account of Indiamen wrecked in the British Isles came from the Goodwin Sands during December 1635 and Plymouth two years later. A great fleet of Dutch ships entered the Downs between Christmas and the New Year, being some 150 in number and all outward bound, some for the East Indies, others the West, the Mediterranean or Rochelle, of which three or four were 'cast away upon the Goodwin', adding to the inestimable treasures and cargo already entombed within the sands. From the west country came news that the *Paulsgrove* of London, belonging to the Honourable East India Company, had been lost on St Nicholas Isle, now known as Drakes Island, Plymouth Sound, during 1637. Returning from the Far East, the *Paulsgrove* put in for fresh water and provisions, advising the company at its London headquarters of its arrival. Letters were sent to her captain instructing him to proceed to London, but unfortunately,

> ... when endeavouring to leave Plymouth, the weather upon the sudden grew exceeding violent, that she could not with safety get out of the Sound. The pilot, purser, and one Thomas Monmouth seeing the danger the ship was in, did entreat the defendant (Captain Cluett) not to proceed, but to return to her former moorings. Defendant being in a fretful mood and passionate humour, threwe downe his staff and stamping said, he would not return. That the Company of the said ship, perceiving the great danger she was in, by prayer committed their souls to

God, and after an hour the carpenters were employed about stopping her hawsers to prevent the seas cominge in too faste uppon the deck, and called for hands to bale the water from the gun deck. Afterwards the cable broke, and the ship was driven ashore.

During the same year that the *Paulsgrove* was lost, the Treasury officials were counting the cost of 'weighing up the *Anne Royal*, sunk at Tilbury Hope, in the Thames'. Built at Deptford in 1587 and launched as the *Ark Raleigh*, she was later renamed *Ark Royal*, then rebuilt at Woolwich in 1608 and her name then changed to *Anne Royal*. Described as a galleon, she was a big ship, of 694 tons (bm), and 55 guns, the biggest of which were 60-pounders. In coming down the Medway in April 1636 an argument had ensued between the Master, Peter White, and the pilot, which resulted in the latter being put ashore. The vessel's main top-sail had then split, but the Master refused to take any action, after which the man o' war stranded, and was later allowed to bilge herself on her own anchor. The total cost of weighing the vessel was an incredible £202,024 0s 5¾d.

Possibly the greatest hoard of sunken treasure still waiting to be found on the seabed around these islands is that which went down in the *Merchant Royal*, of Dartmouth, on 23 September 1641. Returning to England from the Azores, with a king's ransom in treasure captured from the Spanish, her sinking in bad weather was witnessed by another vessel in company which reported the location as 'ten leagues from Land's End' (21 miles). Carrying thirty-six bronze cannon, a crew of eighty and a few passengers under the command of Captain John Timby, in her hold lay '£300,000 in silver, £100,000 in gold, and as much again in jewel'. By present standards of inflation, such a sum must be the twentieth-century equivalent of £20m at least. There were no survivors, and the loss to the Treasury and nation as a whole was of sufficient importance for Samuel Pepys to interrupt proceedings in the House of Commons to communicate the sad news. Meanwhile, public-spirited individuals, intent on breaking some of the traditions and customs associated with the 'right of wreck', were seeking changes in the law, whilst others with self-interest were opposing them. A Frances Bassett wrote to Secretary Nicholas at the Admiralty that:

> I remonstrate against a proposed alteration to the law of salvage, whereby every one who saved wrecked goods was to have a recompense from the proprietors, to be settled if requisite in the Court of Admiralty. The effect of such a regulation would be that the strongest would be the salvors, and that goods would often fall into the hands of poor accountants. The proprietors would never be able to find into whose hands their goods came. The rabble of these sea-borderers possessing that damnable tenet that they had rather trust God with their souls than the Admiralty with their goods.

Having encountered what happened to wreck goods which fell into the hands of their Lordships, the rabble could hardly be blamed for their distrust!

The second half of the seventeenth century saw a far greater number of incidents than the first, including several exceptionally valuable Indiamen, men o' war and the first royal yacht. A very ordinary but different wreck report concerned an incident near Streatley on the River Thames in January 1652. A barge, bringing assorted ammunition to the Tower from Wallingford Castle, was 'drowned' in a lock, and 100 barrels of gunpowder, six tons of slow-match and a further twelve tons of 'bullet' for muskets and pistols was lost. The report concludes with the hope that 'they can weigh up the barge', which must have been a considerable embarrassment sunk in that location.

In 1652, the Heereen XVII, or the seventeen directors on the board of the Dutch United Chartered East India Company (VOC) decided to send seventeen ships to arrive at Batavia the following year, and that between them they should carry a total of 4,200 people and 800,000 guilders-worth of specie and trade goods. By the end of September, with the First Dutch War in progress, it was decided to reduce the specie to 400,000 guilders-worth. A month later, it was decided to send only three ships, each carrying 25,000 guilders in specie. On 1 November 1652, three ships left the Texel for Goeree Roads, an island in the Maas estuary: the 'flute' *Lastdrager*, the 'yacht' *Winthondt*, and the ship *Diamant*. The start of their voyage was hardly auspicious, since on 9 December the yacht was blown ashore on a sandbank, and after discharging her cargo, was abandoned as a total loss. The *Diamant* lost her rudder and was wrecked, whilst the *Lastdrager* drifted over several sandbanks before anchoring, where she lay for three days leaking badly before struggling back to the Texel. After repairs had been carried out, the *Lastdrager* sailed on 9 February 1653 with 206 people aboard, in company with the yacht *Avenhoorn*. On 15 February they passed Fair Isle, being forced to take the northern route around the British Isles due to the state of war between the Dutch and English. But a storm forced them back, and on the twenty-first day since leaving Holland, the *Lastdrager* went on the rocks at Crooks Ayre, Cullivoe Ness, on the island of Yell in the Shetlands. The wreck occurred in a particularly isolated part of Scotland, which encouraged a number of early salvors and 'wrackmen' to try and recover some of the silver coin on board when she sank. One such individual was William Irvine, who attempted to work on her in 1736, and appears to have recovered only one ducatoon and a sixpence, but later attempts were very successful, especially the 1971 expedition to the site, which by using self-contained diving equipment, salvaged a remarkable collection of artefacts and coin.

Eleven years later, the Shetlands were given another Dutch East Indiaman, the *Kennemerland*, a larger and far richer prize than the *Lastdrager*. Purchased by the Amsterdam Chamber of the VOC in 1661 for 33,000 guilders, the *Kennemerland* completed one round trip to the Far East before setting out on her second on 14 December 1664. The vessel destined to accompany her was the *Rijnland*, and between the two of them they loaded 240,000 guilders in specie, in addition to a general cargo and a crew of some 200 each.

The barque *Vega* stranded on the foreshore, Deal, Kent, *c* 1880 *(W. Honey)*

The man o'war *Royal George* sinking at Spithead on 28 August 1782, an accident that cost almost 900 lives, including that of Rear Admiral Kempenfelt *(Schetky – The Tate Gallery)*

The St Ives schooner *Giles Lang*, bound from Porthcawl to Penzance with coal, beached at Maer Lake, Bude, North Cornwall during a gale on 8 November 1896. The interest of the locals can be judged by the size of the crowd! Note the men on the left holding taught a breeches-buoy line to the ship *(Clive Carter collection)*

Stranded on Scarlett Point, Castletown, Isle of Man on 5 September 1892, the excursion paddle-steamer *Mona's Isle* is shown being refloated two days later by the *Tynwald (Ivor Wynne Jones)*

With a state of semi-war existing between the two countries, as with the *Lastdrager*, the northern route was chosen. Running before a southerly gale, but with four lookouts posted in the rigging, they hardly saw breakers before the ship struck the Stoura Stack, a rock pinnacle at the entrance of the Out Skerries natural harbour. In falling, the ship's foremast struck the Stack, offering the means whereby three men, one of whom was the pilot, scrambled ashore. The ship broke in two, the fore part sinking in deep water adjacent to the Stack, the stern being swept along with the tide to be cast up on Bruray Island. The value of such a cargo to the islanders must have been inestimable, and the legend that the locals were drunk for three weeks on the wine and spirits washed ashore is not surprising when one reads a short list of her lading:

> 6 chests of gold and silver, containing 42,000 ducats in gold, and 24,000 guilders in money; 300 pieces of broadcloth; 300 pieces of serge; 40 tuns of brandy; 10 tuns of sack; 10 tuns of French wine; 2 chests of quicksilver; 40 boxes of confections; 20 hogsheads of tobacco; 20 bales of paper; 30,000 weight of pitch and tar; 100 dozen of bridle-bitts and stirrup irons; 30 great guns; sails, cable and anchors.

Whilst this is the list of cargo drawn up by the Crown in its attempt to gain control of the wreck goods, in fact they had overlooked one most important point. The total value of gold and silver quoted was equal to 242,400 guilders, which is approximately in agreement with the figure quoted by the Dutch, *but half of this was on board the Rijnland*, and not, as everyone thought, aboard the *Kennemerland*.

The tenth Earl of Morton, William Douglas, sent Robert Hunter, his Chamberlain, to salvage the wreck. But when news of the incident reached London, the government under Charles II were making strenuous efforts to claim the wreck for themselves, stating:

> All schips belonging to the Kinges enemies ... and cast away upon any of the sea coasts of this Kingdome, and wher of the

saylers . . . or any other persons . . . do survive the loss thereof . . . the schip and all the loading . . . doth belong to his Majestie.

Robert Hunter promised the islanders assisting him in the salvage, 'a fourth of all that shall be won or dragged out of the sea'. On 16 January 1665, three little chests with strong iron bands and double locks were dragged up from the bottom, and were reported to contain 16 bags of gold, another 8 bags, and £2,000 Scots of layed money. The total amount recovered was equal to some 114,200 guilders, which was handed over to Patrick Blair, the Sherriff of the Orkneys and Shetland. Since the Crown were utterly convinced that the wreck held an original 240,000 guilders, they wrongly assumed that the Earl of Morton had somehow secreted the remainder away for himself. This was eventually to lose the Earl his estates. There were in fact some politics behind the scenes, since the wreck incident gave Charles II the long-awaited opportunity to recover the Crown Estates of the outer islands from the Earl, by an Act of Parliament of 27 December 1669. Ownership of the wreck was passed down to Alexander Bruce, the second Earl of Kincardine, and upon his death to the Earl's widow, Dame Veronica de Areskin Von Somersdyke, her heirs and assignees. Following a merger of the Elgin and Kincardine Earldoms in 1747, it is probable that the present Earl of Elgin is the legal owner of the wreck. As with the *Lastdrager*, a number of early salvage attempts were made, several of which were highly successful, and current work being undertaken on the site by amateur divers dates back to its relocation in 1971.

Ten years earlier, in Sussex, there had been a most unusual incident concerning a wreck and bars of silver. A French-owned vessel, the *Mary* of St Malo, which had been taken by an English man o' war as a prize, was offered for sale by auction at Plymouth, having been renamed *Anne* and registered at Dartmouth. After some fierce bidding, Alderman Frederick of London became her new owner for £390, and after spending a further £194 19s 4d on repairs and alterations, sent her on a trading voyage to Alicanti. The price paid for the vessel was abnormally high, since the majority of the bidders were aware of a rumour that one of the French crew, captured with the ship, had stated that there was silver hidden aboard, having been secreted among her frames when the English warship hove in sight. On completion of her first voyage which took her back to London, the *Anne* set out again, but was wrecked on the coast of Barn Shore, East Dean, Sussex. In recompense for saving her cargo, the owner gave the broken hull to the local 'wreckers' for firewood, and it was while she was being broken up that thirteen bars of silver were discovered, of which two were stolen and never seen again. Naturally, Alderman Frederick claimed the bullion for himself, but His Highness's Proctor felt they belonged to the State. Meanwhile summons were issued for the recovery of the missing bars, but to no avail.

The accent to date on East Indiamen losses has centred on the Dutch, although reference has already been made to the Swedish, Danish and French Companies trading in the Far East. On 10 July 1666, a report reached Portsmouth that the English man o' war *Orange*, a 32-gun, 5th-rate vessel of Dutch origin, taken as a prize and entered into the fleet, had captured a French East Indiaman but was forced to sink it near Guernsey, since circumstances prevented it from being sailed back to England. Although the initial report valued her cargo and contents at £1,500,000, a Channel Islander stated that this was a gross underestimate, since one chest alone of precious stones known to be aboard was valued at £40,000, and ambergris and other things were equal to a further £400,000. No record exists of any salvage on the wreck, so her remains probably lie on the seabed near the Channel Isles, awaiting discovery by some future generation of treasure-seekers or salvage divers.

That same winter, a November storm took toll of a great many ships. A Danish vessel put into Peterhead harbour reporting that both his Admiral and Vice Admiral's ships had gone down with no survivors; the *Crown of England*, a

Scots craft worth £4,000, was wrecked on Coquet Island; a French ship carrying salt and packs of linen at Banff; another 'cast-away' in Shetland. In North Wales, a Flemish ship with 600 'pieces' of Spanish wine was found ashore with not a living soul aboard, whilst the *St Peter* of Ostend ended up on the rocks near Plymouth. Her cargo of wine and brandy was recovered intact, unlike the tobacco, sugar and beaver skins contained in one of the eleven ships in convoy from New England and New York. A south-west gale had put her ashore near St Nicholas Isle, and but for their impatience to resume passage for London they would all have been at anchor in the Hamoaze, and safe from the gales. Meanwhile, in Tenby, in what was then Pembrokeshire, a vessel of 400 tons and another carrying beaver skins were also reported as wrecked.

Another shipwreck of the period, which has become well known subsequent to its relocation in the 1960s, was the Genoese vessel *Santo Christo de Castello*, known affectionately today as the 'Mullion Pin Wreck', after the site yielded countless domestic brass pins. Although from the same stables as the many Dutch East Indiamen already mentioned, the '*Santo Christo*' had been built in the same Amsterdam yards but with finance provided by a group of Genoese merchants. The passport requested of King Charles II, was for the ship to proceed on a normal trading voyage from her birthplace to Genoa, calling at Lisbon, Cadiz and possibly other ports in Spain. On 15 September 1667 she arrived in Carrick Roads, Falmouth, a 500-ton vessel, valued at £50,000, with 120 crew plus passengers, and her hold packed full of lead ingots, iron, clothes, spices, domestic pins, thimbles, candlesticks, tobacco goods and other valuable manufactured items. Exactly how long she remained at Falmouth is uncertain, but on 3 October she appeared off Mullion at anchor. For two days she remained there, then the wind changed, her cables parted and she went ashore, beam on to a ledge of rocks at the mouth of Polglas Cove, near Polurrian. Twenty-five people drowned, the remainder, including her captain, Lorenzo Viviano, managed to reach the shore, despite towering cliffs over the site. A considerable quantity of cinnamon, cloves, and coral was salvaged, followed by iron, lead, guns, anchors and cables, Russian hides, masts, beams and furniture, most of which was taken into custody by Sir Francis Godolphin, the Vice Admiral for Cornwall. The goods lay under lock and key so long that 'the charge of keeping the same for warehouse roome and looking to it doth daily increase, and the cynnamon and hides are grown worse, and deteriorated by their long lying undisposed of', according to William Painter of Sithney, gent.

Considering the general lack of detail recorded concerning shipwrecks, it is a refreshing change to find some smattering of human interest in a report of 28 March 1667 from Swansea. The source is the Domestic State Papers, which state,

> The vessel stranded at Laugharne, in Carmarthenshire, proves to be the *Justice* of Stade (on the Elbe, near Hamburg); a small quantity of her wine and brandy, and her crew of twelve men and boys are saved. A Tenby vessel from Bristol was bulged within the bar, and in great danger. The captain bade a Quaker woman in the cabin, who was afraid, lay her head on two great books; she asked what they were, and being told they were church bibles said it was no wonder such a violent storm fell upon them, and it would cease when those Jonahs were cast overboard; but coming on shore in a boat, with others, she alone was drowned, and proved the Jonah.

Another strange story from the same source concerns witches,

> November 2 1667, Harwich, from Captain Silas Taylor. They tell a strange story at Ipswich of one of their ships that was lost in the late storms; that another ship of the same town passing by them and being well acquainted, they sent their remembrances to friends; the master Jonathan Banticke, to his parents; one Hornegild, a passenger who had lost his ship at Scarborough Road, his love to his wife and children, and all the other seamen to their relatives. When asked the reason and whether their ship was leaky, or what they wanted, the first ship replied that they had long laboured to free their maintop

where sat a couple of witches, but by all they could do, could not remove nor get them down, and so they were lost people. The master named the two witches to the second ships master and his company, insomuch that they are now in prison in Ipswich. The story is credibly reported by the second ship and generally believed. Many light vessels pass by to the north and laden ships to the south. I hope the price of coal will fall apace.

Although several references to the frequency of ship losses around the British Isles have been made, the wrecks mentioned to date have been spasmodic, and in numbers far from representative of the true story. Only by making reference to every known loss in a definite period of time, is the appalling waste of ships and men brought home to us all. Chosen entirely at random, the months of January and February 1668 serve to make this point. Before proceeding to relate the shipwrecks reported, the weather must be considered. During the seventeenth century, it was the practice for a monthly return to be made to the Admiralty of all the King's and merchant ships anchored in the Downs. The same report also gave the wind direction, but not its strength, so that only an intelligent interpretation of direction and the actual numbers of ships in the Downs gives some indication of conditions at sea. At the end of December 1667, from the 24th to 31st the wind was predominantly westerly, with three men o' war in the Downs for the whole period, and the numbers of merchant vessels rose from five on Christmas Eve to twenty-nine on the 26th, and reached forty-four by the last day of the month. The following represent the known losses, in chronological order, for the next two months:

Date		Place	Details
January	2	Pembroke	Ostend prize, ashore near Tenby
1668	6	Carmarthen	St Malo vessel, ashore on Laugharne Sand
	9	Yarmouth	Several vessels cast away near Yarmouth
	10	Newcastle	Fly-boat of London, cast away under castle

Date		Place	Details
	10	Pembroke	The Ostend prize was lost at New Marsh
	15	Padstow	English vessel from Lisbon cast away
	16	Swansea	*Joseph* of Rochelle, cast on shore here
	21	Scillies	French vessel bilged in harbour and sold
	23	Medway	Medway above Upnor cleared of wrecks, *Helverson* cleared from wreck on which she sank; orders wanted regarding *Guelder de Ruyter* and *Vanguard* (still sunk)
	30	Harwich	Vessel aground on the Ridge, 70t of coal
	31	Holy Is.	Scotch privateer ashore near Holy Island
February	1	Blackwall	*Leister* wreck bought at Blackwall
1668	4	not known	Vessel belonging to Thomas Long is lost
	4	Newcastle	Fly-boat ashore on Black Middings
	5	Rye	Timber laden hoy of London, cast away
	7	Bridlington	Vessel ashore near this place
	9	Portsmouth	*Slothany*, sunken vessel now weighed
	12	Yarmouth	Fly-boat in collision and sunk, two maids asleep between decks perished
	20	Portsmouth	Owner of sunken vessel will not come
	21	Bigbury Bay	A Venetian and Genoese both lost in bay
	22	Portland	Great storms—Dutchman ashore on beach
	23	Bridlington	Small collier cast away in the Bay
	24	Dublin	Merchant ship in harbour driven ashore and two or three others bilged
	29	Winchelsea	French ship lost off castle, all drowned

Whilst it might appear that a yacht has no place in a history of shipwreck, there was one such vessel lost in 1675 which should not be ignored. This was the *Mary*, the very first of the royal yachts used by English monarchs, presented to Charles II by the Dutch when he was restored to the throne in 1660. Today, the term 'yacht' signifies a small pleasure craft, of a particular type and size, but in the mid-1600s the expression was used to describe a light, fast, and very seaworthy craft, luxuriously appointed for the transportation of royalty and nobles. The word 'yacht' is derived from the Dutch *ter jacht Gaen*, meaning 'to go a-hunting'. It was during the return journey from exile, between Breda and Rotterdam, that Charles II went aboard a yacht for the first time. His obvious pleasure and admiration prompted Van Vlooswick, Burgomaster of Amsterdam, to offer His Royal Highness the gift of another, similar craft. The *Mary* was purchased from the Dutch Board of Admiralty, and arrived in this country on 12 August 1660. Although she enjoyed a period of fame as the King's plaything, after only a very brief career as this nation's first royal yacht the *Mary* was replaced by an English-built craft, with a greater draught, more suitable for these waters, the original being given to the fleet as a 'packet' vessel. Her last voyage commenced in Dublin, and she sailed for Chester with a total of seventy-four people aboard, consisting of twenty-eight crew, the Earl of Ardglass, the Earl of Meath, who was accompanied by his son, Lord Ardee, as well as forty-three other passengers. In dense fog, she struck an outlying rock on the Out Skerries, seven miles from Holyhead, Anglesey. Had her very tall single mast not formed a bridge with the rocks as she listed, possibly a great many more than thirty-five lives would have been lost, which incidentally included the Earl of Meath, the captain and bosun. When the *Mary* first arrived in this country, her sole armament consisted of two ornamental bronze guns, specially cast in Amsterdam, but such a vessel demanded more than just two cannon, and a matching set of a further eight were ordered from the Tower of London, and fitted in 1661. For 296 years the remains of the *Mary* lay undisturbed, reduced now to a great heap of ballast, intermingled with the ten bronze guns, until in 1971 two groups of amateur divers located the wreck on the same day.

The same year as the redundant royal yacht was lost, a dozen or more other vessels of some size were also wrecked, most of

The steamer *Gipsy*, which got across the tide in the River Avon, below Bristol, and broke in two at low water, 1878 *(National Maritime Museum)*

Within twenty-four hours of coming ashore during an easterly gale, the *Kergall* was completely destroyed; this picture shows her fuel tank embedded deep in sand, and her engine room fittings *(Eric Collins collection)*

The French pitwood schooner *Olympe*, wrecked in Gunwalloe Church Cove, south Cornwall, 3 October 1910 *(F.E. Gibson)*

them in the west country. On 10 February, the *Johanna and Sarah* of Boston, New England, 120 tons and four guns, was wrecked on the 'Deadman, near Foy' (ie the Dodman, near Fowey). On 26 March the 350-ton, twenty-six gun *Arms of Bristol* was wrecked near Ilfracombe. On the Goodwin Sands, the Deal and Walmer fishermen received rough treatment from the Dutch crew of the *St Tobys*, who had gone out to assist when she stranded on 31 March. Several of them were cut and stabbed by knives and swords when they attempted to board, the sailors fearing for their lives. Five months later, no doubt the same fishermen were present at the *Florentine*, an armed merchantman of fourteen guns, whose masts were all that showed above the surface of the sands on 25 August. In her hold there were said to be some 30 tons of lead, in 200lb ingots. The month of December saw the end of at least a dozen vessels, amongst which were a 100-ton Bordeaux ship on the Lizard; the *Port Morant Merchant* within three leagues of Bristol; a vessel carrying chestnuts in Bude Bay, Cornwall; a large ship in the Isles of Scilly; a Dutchman under the Citadel at Plymouth; and between Bristol and Newport a vessel carrying elephants' tusks. Meanwhile, in the coastal villages around Mount's Bay, Cornwall, the talk centred on the Bordeaux fleet, 'which were cast away in the bay, so many that the writer could not give their number. The general discourse in these parts is nothing but wreck'.

The closing years of the seventeenth century were to be remembered by the Admiralty, if no-one else, since between 1689 and 1691 they lost three major men o' war and one frigate, as well as a number of smaller craft. A six-gun fire-ship, the *Charles & Henry*, 120 tons, was lost close to Plymouth on 29 November 1689. On Christmas Day the *Centurion*, thirty-four guns, 513 tons (bm), and the sixty-two gun *Henrietta* (the latter having been built as the *Langport* and renamed in 1660), were both wrecked on Mount Batten. Tragic though these disasters may have been, they were all eclipsed by the sinking of the *Coronation*, compared to which the simultaneous stranding of the *Harwich* in Plymouth Sound was relatively trivial. On patrol in the English Channel, hoping to lure the French into action, the fleet turned back for Plymouth on 2 September 1691, with a south-east gale almost dead astern. The entrance to the Sound was far from distinct, with Penlee Point and the Mewstone partially obscured by mist, so that the majority of the ships anchored off Rame Head. The *Northumberland* and the *Harwich* both got inside the Sound under reefed topsails, but the combination of tide and wind drove the former ashore in the Hamoaze, and the *Harwich* on to Mount Edgcumbe, not far from what is known today as Drake's Island, then St Nicholas. The *Northumberland* found herself a soft berth, the *Harwich* was finally broken up where she lay in the shallows, and the *Royal Oak*, ashore nearby, and within sight of Mount Edgcumbe House, was saved only after all her guns had been lifted out to lighten her.

Meanwhile, a mile offshore from the Rame, at least twenty-five ships were heaving at their anchors, catching brief glimpses of the land between rain storms, and each ship's captain wondering how long his cables would stand the strain. The *Coronation*, a 2nd-rate ship-of-the-line (Captain Skelton), began to drag towards the shore. Her difficulties may well have been aggravated by a small prize vessel said to have been secured alongside. She was seen to have a heavy list to port, and shortly afterwards all her masts were cut down in an attempt to reduce their windage or drag, and possibly assist her to regain an even keel. What happened next will never be known, since she suddenly rolled over and disappeared beneath the surface. She carried a crew of over 600, in addition to two companies of Royal Marines. But the survivors, some of whom reached shore on wreckage and others in a long boat, were reported as few as five, or by others as twenty-two—an appalling loss of life so close to shore. The wreck site (or possibly the two parts of the site) was relocated by local divers between 1967 and 1977 some half a mile apart. The inshore wreck site was the first to be discovered, but not one single artefact was found which could tie it to the *Corona-tion*, other than the circumstantial evidence of over fifty iron cannon, and no other known shipwreck likely to have carried this amount of armament. Offshore, half a mile due south, in 60ft of water, seventeen more cannon and three anchors are without doubt part of the bow section of the *Coronation*, since trapped in the bottom was a large pewter plate, which on cleaning revealed the most positive evidence of all, the personal crest of Captain Charles Skelton. The relocation of this offshore section took many months, and that is not surprising, despite the twenty-five surviving log books each of which give an eyewitness account of the sinking and its location! The variations in the positions described are almost unbelievable; the *Albermarle* gave it as 'half way between Ramhead and the Eddystone', the *Burford* said it was 'lost to the westward of the Rame', *Flame* stated that it 'foundered in Plymouth Sound', *Ossory* insisted she 'saw the wreck on shore', and the *Windsor Castle*'s officers in three logbooks respectively recorded that it 'sank half a mile off Ramehead', 'overset three miles from shore' and 'sank about two miles off Rame'. The site was found three-quarters of a mile from the land, and the only logical explanation can surely be that on capsizing, her deck guns, anchors, ship's bell, ready-use shot and the contents of the galley all fell out, while the hull then drifted ashore, to break up in the shallows.

3

POOR ENGLAND HAS LOST
SO MANY MEN

1700–1749

Except for the World Wars of the twentieth century, more British seamen and ships of the navy were lost in the 1700s, than in any comparable period of this nation's history. Predominantly, ships of war and not merchant vessels were involved, and of these more than half were lost by storm or accident, and not battle.

It was exactly 8.35 am on 19 September 1700, when the 700-ton man o' war *Carlisle* blew up in the Downs, off Kent. The entire ship was lifted up out of the sea, as if by some giant hand, then fell back, and, according to eyewitness accounts, appeared to disintegrate. Richard Hitchcock, a seaman serving on board as the gunner's servant, was at the mizzen topmast head of the frigate, taking down the ship's pennant when the accident occurred. As the ship exploded with a tremendous roar beneath him, rattling the windows in Ramsgate some 4 miles distant, the townsfolk ran into the streets convinced that they were under attack. Hitchcock was blown clean off his lofty perch and fell into the sea, fortunately clear of all wreckage, one of only four survivors from the 128 men known to have been aboard. Her normal complement was 164 officers and men, but of these Captain Francis Dove, the senior gunner Christopher Short, the carpenter James Oswald, the surgeon William Hapton, the purser the Rt Hon Burton, as well as seamen and marines, were all on shore. Others off ship when she exploded were the boat's crew, who had just left the boom to row to Ramsgate to pick up their captain, only minutes before the disaster.

The cause of the explosion was never clearly established, but it was assumed that a seaman had been in the magazine stealing gunpowder, a practice not uncommon at the time. Prior to the peace of Ryswick in 1697, English men o' war carried a 'yeoman of the powder room', responsible, under the gunner, for all explosive materials carried on board. Only the ship's gunner and his yeoman were ever allowed in the magazine, but as an economy measure, the Admiralty discontinued the appointment. It is interesting that the position was re-established, and such a rating appeared on the books of all warships in home waters, and, in due course, overseas, from 26 September 1700—the very day before the court martial concerning the loss of the *Carlisle* was convened on board the frigate *Hampshire*, at anchor in the Downs.

A subsequent survey of the wreck by Trinity House was carried out at the request of the Admiralty, who sought not only its exact location, but also its condition before any possible salvage commenced. Their report dated 11 October 1700 reads as follows:

We having with all exactness we were capable of at this time and season, sounded upon and about the said wreck, do humbly report to their Lordships that the said wreck lies in about seven fathoms at low water. The ground, a kind of blue clay with a few stones on the top of it, with her stern to the southward, and lying North and by West, and South and by East, the South Foreland bearing South and by West ½ West, and the North Foreland, North and by West. The leading mark to find the wreck is to keep the Upper Deal windmill a little open to the southward of the castle. The thwart mark is a reddish brick stable at the North end of the town, which is to be kept half a ships length open to the southward of a windmill standing up in the country, called Wingeham Hill.

That the after part of the said wreck as far forward as the bulkhead of the quarterdeck, we judge to remain whole, the taffrail being but four feet underwater at a low ebb. The rest of the ship forward, we believe to be blown apart, excepting the floors and some of the futtocks, which do remain about twelve feet above the ground. That the said wreck, in the position and posture it is at present, must needs be dangerous to ships passing into and out of the Downs, as lying in the best of the Road. That it may be expected the sea and the tides, if it happens to blow hard from the North or South upon spring tides will, in some short time, break away the upper works at least of the said wreck as it hath, in a manner, wholly done those of the merchantmen sunk by the storm in the year 1689/90 though some remains thereof, or of some others, are sometimes met with by those that sweep for anchors, which must doubtless cut or damnify the cables of ships lying in the Road.

That the after part of the wreck which yet sits whole, or at least the upper works may be blown up, which in our opinion ought to be done as soon as maybe, and that the bottom, or what part afterwards remains, may be swept, and being lifted as it may, by four vessels of about 100 tons each, may be carried into shoal water. And when that is done, if not before, her guns and cables may undoubtedly be taken up in a proper season of the year. But what the charge of blowing up or weighing the said wreck as proposed, it is impossible to make any reasonable calculation of, since there is no answering for the weather or other accidents that may attend a work of this nature. In the meantime, a distinguishable buoy be laid on the broadside of the wreck, if not one on each side.

As will be seen in Chapter 4, in the late 1790s, the 5th-rate man o' war *Amphion* also exploded in equally mysterious circumstances. The cause was again presumed to be the theft of gunpowder, but both cases lacked positive evidence. Not so, however, in the case of the seventy-gun *Exeter*, which also blew up in the Hamoaze, Plymouth, on 13 September 1691. At the time she was hove down alongside a careening hulk, in order to effect repairs to her hull sheathing. Her guns, shot, and 200 barrels of gunpowder were all supposed to be out of the ship, and safely ashore in the dockyard cellars, but her gunner had secreted twenty barrels for himself beneath the forecastle, which unfortunately was the scene of a fire, when the galley timbers caught alight by accident. Over 100 men died in the blaze and explosion, and after being completely gutted, the *Exeter* sank. Among the survivors found swimming in the river was the gunner, who was immediately chained hand and foot, and thrown into jail to await trial.

Bad weather has always been the main cause of the majority of shipwrecks, but the outcome of the Great Storm of 1703 was unprecedented. Broadsheets and early newspaper reports concerning gales and bad weather were often couched in such poetic and eloquent language that it was impossible to make any reliable comparisons. Nevertheless, the storm that struck the British Isles and the Low Countries of Holland and Flanders in the November of that year may well have seen no equal, either before or since. One witness described it as 'the greatest, longest, and most severe storm that ever the world saw', which must not be taken too seriously, since the strength and fury of tropical cyclones and their equivalents never reach our northern latitudes. But without doubt, in the experience and memory of the British nation, none could recall any storm to equal that which has been passed down in history simply as 'the Great Storm'.

The eighteen months prior to November 1703 had seen severe weather-pattern disturbances, with poor grain harvests in 1702, fruit stripped off the trees by gales and heavy rain and widespread flooding. The duration of the Great Storm, which amounted to a series of severe gales, was nineteen days, of which thirteen in particular—those between Friday 19 November and Wednesday 31 November—were the worst, with the climax about Thursday 25 November. On land, in Kent alone over a thousand dwelling houses and barns were completely flattened. In the chronicle of Daniel Defoe, to whom we are indebted for a full account of the storm, he admits to attempting to count the number of trees blown down in the county, but gave up at 17,000! Elsewhere, the story was much the same. Parts of Yorkshire and Lincoln suffered minor earthquakes, chimneystacks fell in their thousands, roofs stripped of thatch and tiles. The Bishop of Bath and Wells was killed in his bed when a chimneystack fell through his roof, and Queen Anne was taken to a cellar under St James's Palace for safety. Sheet lead covering the roof of

Westminster Abbey was blown clean off, whilst that on the roof of the Admiralty was rolled back, like some gigantic carpet. Oxfordshire experienced a number of waterspouts, which ripped through this part of rural England, uprooting trees and haystacks. Four hundred windmills were destroyed, and in the Severn Valley some 15,000 sheep drowned in the floodwaters.

No part of the British Isles escaped the devastation, and from the coast and at sea came the worst news of all; so many seamen were lost that starving families could be counted in their thousands. It was Queen Anne who suggested to the Admiralty that any seaman who perished in the storm should be treated as if he had lost his life in action against the enemy, hence allowing their families some relief from public funds. When finally the full picture of death and destruction emerged, and was placed before the monarch, the Queen decreed that 19 January 1704 was to be a day of public fasting, in memory of those who had lost their lives. As far as is known, this was a unique decree, one which has never been repeated to this day.

At sea conditions must have been indescribable. Apart from the appalling loss of ships and seamen, the Great Storm will always be associated with the destruction of the Eddystone lighthouse, along with its designer and builder, Henry Winstanley, and his crew. Vessels on the south and east coasts bore the brunt of the weather, and an eyewitness account of events in the Downs was recorded by James Adams, who was passenger aboard a merchantman at anchor, awaiting an improvement in the weather before proceeding to Portsmouth, and on to Lisbon. Severe gales lashed the coast for three whole days without cease from 19 November, after which the wind moderated and generally everyone was convinced the worst was over. About 23 November the gales returned, blowing from south to south-east, increasing steadily in their fury, being at least of hurricane force from the south-south-west on the 26th, and reaching a climax between 3 and 7 am on Saturday 27 November. Caught at sea in the English Channel during the early phase, the apparent three-day calm caused even seamen as experienced as Sir Cloudesley Shovell to bring his fleet of men o' war into the Downs to anchor.

As the wind changed direction and began to increase again, making the Goodwin Sands a lee shore, so several of the warship captains slipped their cables and put to sea, rather than risk being blown ashore. One vessel, an unidentified Dutch craft, sailed over part of the North Goodwin sandbank, became stranded and was lost with all hands. Next day, some of the same warships returned to the Downs, when the wind quickly reached full gale force, and continued to increase until it was inconceivable that it could get any worse. All the ships struck their topmasts to reduce 'windage', put out an extra anchor, put their best cables end to end, and put their trust in God. On the smaller vessels, such as the merchantman which carried James Adams, whole seas rolled clean over them, and a great many foundered from the sheer weight of water. During the early hours of 27 November, in pitch darkness, ships began to drag or else their cables parted. Most were forced to cut away their masts completely to reduce top weight, but by 2 am almost every vessel was adrift. Distress guns boomed out in vain, from the North to the South Foreland, but it was a case of every vessel and man for themselves. Adams witnessed the *Northumberland* and the *Mary* both disappear as they went on the Goodwin Sands, but seemingly missed the destruction of the *Restoration*, which, although of comparable tonnage, may have been obscured by driving rain.

The *Northumberland*, a seventy-gun 3rd-rate, commanded by Captain Greenaway, was wrecked with the loss of her entire crew of 253 men. Slightly larger, the sixty-gun *Mary*, originally the *Speaker* of fifty guns, also went to pieces on the sandbank, taking Rear Admiral Beaumont and 272 crew to a watery grave. Her captain, Edward Hopson, and the purser, were the only two men ashore, and hence the only survivors from among the officers. But a seaman, Thomas Atkins, had a most remarkable escape. As the *Mary* struck bottom, Atkins was washed overboard, but managed to cling to some floating wreckage. A freak wave then picked him up, depositing him on the upper deck of the *Stirling Castle*, another seventy-gun, 3rd-rate man o' war, also adrift and about to go ashore. As she grounded, so the sea flung the seaman overboard for a second time, to fall providentially into the one remaining ship's boat which had broken adrift from its lashings on deck. In it, Atkins eventually reached the shore, almost unconscious and suffering from exposure. The *Stirling Castle*, like so many others that night, became a total wreck, but seventy survived from her crew of 349, amongst whom were her 3rd Lieutenant, chaplain, surgeon's mate, and four marine officers. *Restoration* went to a watery grave unseen, with not one survivor out of 386 crew, and it was not for several days that her shattered hulk was found by fishermen half buried in the Goodwins, from which they recovered the body of Captain Fleetwood Emes, her commanding officer.

No doubt terrified by the storm and scenes of destruction all round him, Adams nevertheless took the trouble to record all he had seen in a diary, but it was several weeks later before its contents reached those in authority. The ship in which Adams was borne, had already cut away her masts before the *Stirling Castle* was wrecked. Fearing that she might drag her anchors or the cables part, the crew slipped both hawsers, and with only a tarpaulin lashed to the stump of the mizzen to give some steerage way, she headed for the open sea. They were blown north for four days, with no idea as to their position, until they encountered a pilot boat, whose crew assisted them to a nearby Norwegian port. Repairs took several weeks, after which the ship and Adams returned to the Downs, and later resumed their original voyage to Portugal.

During those terrible days, four major men o' war were lost on the Goodwins, with an estimated 1,190 lives. A great many more might have been saved had the Deal and Walmer boatmen not been more interested in 'wrecking' than in human life. Survivors from the wrecks could clearly be seen on the

Goodwins at low water, but it was not until the Mayor of Deal, Thomas Powell, seized a number of local boats by force and made their crews go out to the sands, that some of the seamen were saved. In Yarmouth Roads, Norfolk, the forty-eight gun *Reserve*, having returned from Russian convoy duties only two days before, was swamped by huge seas whilst at anchor and sank with a further 258 drowned; the *Vigo* and bomb vessel *Mortar* were blown on to the coast of Holland and wrecked with eight men lost. At Selsey, the advise boat *Eagle* was amongst the victims, also the sixty-gun *Resolution* off Beachy Head, fortunately without loss of a single life. But the *Newcastle*, lost near Chichester, and the *Canterbury*, lost near Bristol, between them added a further 255 to the death toll. Other victims included the *Portsmouth* at the Nore, the *Vanguard* which oversett at Chatham, bringing the total of men o' war to thirteen, and lives lost as a consequence over 2,000. Of merchant ships lost, there is no reliable record; 'hundreds' were said to have been blown from Execution Dock to Limehouse in the Thames, where they were jammed together and smashed to firewood, while above London Bridge 500 wherries and sixty barges were sunk. At Grimsby, almost every vessel in harbour was blown out to sea, and twenty never returned, and at Plymouth three merchantmen were sunk in the Cattewater. Of the 160 ships known to have been at anchor in the Downs on 26 November, only seventy were accounted for next day, while wrecks were floating bottom up everywhere.

Had not the bulk of the English Channel fleet escaped to sea safely during the early hours of 27 November, the outcome to the navy could well have been catastrophic, with the certain addition to the 'lost list' of the *Prince George*, 2nd rate; *Essex*, 3rd rate; *Shrewsbury*, 2nd rate; *Eagle*, 3rd rate; *Content*, 3rd rate; *Chatham*, 4th rate; *Assistance*, 2nd rate; *Mary*, galley, and fireship *Hunter*. A merciful providence may well have saved the lives of a further 3,000 seamen that night, and certain events suggest that fate was cheated of the loss of two major, and one minor warship, since the *Association*,

Eagle and *Firebrand* escaped, only to come to grief together on the Isles of Scilly, four years later. In fact, following the Great Storm, the Admiralty were utterly convinced that the *Association* was amongst the lost ships, since nothing was heard of her until 23 January 1704, fifty-eight days later. At the height of the storm, she was at anchor off the Long Sand Head, near Harwich, when both cables parted. The wind drove her clean over the tail of the Galloper Sand, where there was less than 12ft of water under her keel, and in fact she struck the bottom several times. Several gunports were stove in by the sea, as was the main entering port, and she lost her rudder. With no mainmast, only a scrap of sail, and her rigging a total mess, *Association* managed to limp into Gottenberg, in Sweden, and a further twenty-eight crew were to die of sickness before she reappeared off Chatham, much to everyone's surprise.

It was another less severe gale that brought about the premature end of the thirty-two-gun, 5th-rate *Hastings*, during the night of 9/10 February 1707. Accompanied by the *Margate*, a twenty-four-gun 6th-rate, built as the *Jersey*, the two men o' war left Yarmouth Roads, Norfolk, as escorts for a fleet of 100 merchantmen, bound for Holland. The wind veered into the north-east quarter, increasing to a full gale, so that the convoy was obliged to put back. *Hastings*, in the van, struck on Scroby Sand, and within half an hour turned over, and only about thirty men escaped the wreck.

The catastrophe of 22 October 1707, in which four warships, some 2,000 men, and a leading Admiral were lost by shipwreck amongst the Isles of Scilly, off Cornwall, left the nation stunned. With an Admiralty still counting the cost of replacing ships and men lost in the Great Storm, to lose even more during what was after all a routine 'passage' from Gibraltar to Portsmouth, was an unprecedented disaster. It was of course, sheer coincidence that of the five vessels involved, three had narrowly escaped the elements together four years earlier, but in an age when superstition was rife, seamen made much of the incident.

On 29 September 1707, twenty-one men o' war, including four fireships, were at anchor in Gibraltar harbour, preparing to leave for England. All that summer the fleet had harassed the French in the Mediterranean, destroying a large percentage of their ships, as well as laying siege to Toulon, although the extensive bombardment of the port had been largely ineffectual, thanks to the vast earth works thrown up around the town. But winter was now close at hand, and October was no time to have ninety-gun ships at sea, with no established base or dockyard to which to turn for shelter or repair during the stormy months ahead. On board the *Association* (and not for the first time) was the Admiral and Commander-in-Chief of the Mediterranean Fleet, and Rear Admiral of Great Britain, Sir Cloudesley Shovell. He was accompanied on board by a select entourage, mostly relatives by marriage: Sir John Narborough and his brother James, sons of Lady Shovell by her first husband; Henry Trelawney, second son of the Bishop of Winchester, while *Association*'s captain, Edmund Loades, was Lady Shovell's nephew. A favourite of Queen Anne, now rich and famous after a lifetime's service in the navy, Sir Cloudesley originated from an obscure Norfolk hamlet of Cock Thorpe, which in itself has a remarkable history. From each of the 'three humble dwellings, or rather hovels', to quote one source, came boys who were to become famous admirals, namely, Sir Cloudesley Shovell, Sir John Narborough and Sir Christopher Mimms, whilst less than a mile away, at Burnham Thorpe, a vicarage saw the birth of Viscount Nelson.

Preparations completed, the fleet of twenty-one ships headed out into the Atlantic, then north for the English Channel and home. By 21 October it was thought they were at the entrance to the Channel, but successive gales had set them way off course, and eventually the entire fleet hove to in order to take lead-line soundings of depth, an admission that they were lost. Conflicting accounts exist of events that day, and whether or not a meeting of the fleet's sailing masters took place on board the flagship, but it is reasonably certain from surviving log-book evidence that no such event occurred. The soundings varied from 55 fathoms (330ft), to 145 fathoms (870ft), after which the lead ships, *Lennox*, *Valeur* and *Phoenix*, were detached to proceed direct to Falmouth for convoy duties.

At 8 pm on 22 October 1707 the *Association* struck the Outer Gilstone, almost on the extreme south-western edge of the Isles of Scilly, and since there were no survivors, it must be presumed she went to pieces very quickly. Following astern, the *St George* struck the same rocks, losing part of her stern gallery, but managed to get clear. The *Eagle*, the *Romney* and the *Firebrand* were not so fortunate. The seventy-gun *Eagle* ran over Tearing Ledge, close to the Bishop rock, now the site of a famous lighthouse, and sank in 130ft of water. As for the *Romney*, either her site has yet to be found, or else it is the confused assortment of pieces of wreck, mixed with others, in the vicinity of Rosevear Ledges, but there is no uncertainty regarding the *Firebrand's* resting place. She found her way along the southern side of the Western Rocks, finally sinking between Annet and St Agnes Islands, whilst the *Phoenix* was run ashore in an inlet between Tresco and St Martins.

The finding of the wrecks in 1967, and subsequent salvage of a vast fortune in silver and gold coin is too well documented to justify repetition, but recent research has cast some light on the original source of the specie. First and foremost, although the *Association* was not a treasure ship, but merely a man o' war on her routine duties, it was an accepted practice and valuable perquisite of captains and admirals to carry specie and bullion around the world. In fact, warships, because of the obvious security they offered, often carried vast sums between governments or banks, in return for which the commanding officer concerned often received as much as two and a half percent of the gross value, at no expense or risk other than the performance of his normal duty. The Portuguese gold coins found on both the *Association* and *Eagle* sites were specie shipped by Lisbon bankers for London, but unfortunately the total sum involved remains unknown. Of the other coin aboard, a certain sum would have been what was termed the 'Queen's plate', ie the sum carried on board all ships, to purchase provisions, pay the odd bribe, entertainment cost and general emergencies, in much the same way that modern warships often carry gold sovereigns for just the same purpose. In addition, there would be personal sums of money, belonging to the officers and 'gentlemen', and no doubt lesser sums amongst the seamen as well. Finally, there was the balance of regimental funds of the Coldstream Guards Regiments of Foot. This money was never intended for the *Association's* safe keeping, having been destined for another, unnamed warship, commanded by a Captain Elwes. A last-minute change of plans sent that particular vessel direct to Lisbon, and hence the specie was entrusted to the flagship. Colonel Andrew Bissett, as Commander-in-Chief of the Regiments, had recently been at the Battle of Almanza, in northern Spain. Taking it upon himself to make up the Regimental accounts, he sent sufficient money on board *Association* to cover the cost of recruiting, training and equipping three new Companies, to replace losses in the field. Upon hearing of its loss in the subsequent wreck, the Paymaster General of Goods and Garrisons (Home) approached the Lords of the Treasury for reimbursement, only to be told, 'There is no provision for losses of this kind.'

It must not be assumed that all the shipwrecks or losses of the early 1700s were solely English men o' war, nor that the East India Companies had ceased to lose ships. The night of 7/8 November 1711 found the Dutch East India ship *De Liefde (The Love)*, running north before a severe southerly gale, somewhere off the extreme northern coast of Scotland. Outward bound from the Texel, on her fourth and last voyage to Batavia, the instructions issued in Amsterdam to her captain, Barent Muijkens, were that on no account was he to risk his command or the specie carried, by passing through the Straits of Dover. Instead, he was to take the longer but safer northern route, passing down the west coast of Ireland.

Although well armed with forty guns and professional Company troops, as part of the 300 persons aboard, the 'Gentlemen Seventeen', as the Directors of the VOC were known, were not prepared to risk the possible piracy of the 227,000 guilders she carried. Neither did *De Liefde* sail alone, since she was in company with the *Cockenge* and the *Mossel*, but all three became separated in the bad weather. During the early hours of a Sunday morning, *De Liefde* crashed into a steep cliff face on the south-west tip of a group of islands known as the Out Skerries, some fifteen miles north-east of Lerwick, in the Shetland Isles. In the Dutch records, *De Liefde* is recorded as having been lost on a reef called 'Mioni', (in Dutch 'Uutscheren'), not far from the coast of 'Hitland'. The financial loss was considerable to the Company, and early the following January they entered into a contract with a Dutchman named Wybe Wybrants, of Friesland, to salvage all he could, especially the treasure. He arrived on site with the galliots *Otter* and *Arent* on 28 April, but reported that he could find nothing at the site except for some rigging. Others who followed in his footsteps were more successful, including Captain Rowe and John Lethbridge who between them salvaged a great deal of money and fittings. The wreck site was relocated in 1964 by naval divers from the minehunter HMS *Shoulton*, who salvaged a considerable number of coins; since then *De Liefde* has become almost infamous for the adverse publicity and general difficulties which the recovery of her specie has brought about between different salvage groups. Other Dutch East Indiamen wrecked on Shetland, or which foundered in the immediate vicinity and have yet to be found, include *Zeepard* (1665); *Tobian Leijdsman* (1688); *Pijlswaard* (1690); *Capelle* (1690); *Hetland Van Schouwen* (1690); *Alkmaar* (1690); *Rijnenburg* (1713); and the *Nieuw Vyvervreugd* (1756).

State Treasury Papers for the early part of the eighteenth century are full of fascinating references to shipwreck, diving, salvage, and wrecking in general. A brief glimpse of the period 1700–1730 reveals such information as 'permission to fish

74

Following collision five miles offshore from Selsey Bill in dense fog on 21 June 1979, between the MV *Tarpenbek* and the navy auxiliary RFA *Sir Geraint*, the former sank, leaving her bows afloat. Four days later she rolled over and capsized, but was eventually refloated and righted, before being towed to Rotterdam for repair *(HMS Daedalus SAR Flight)*

The scene from Manacles Point, St Keverne, Cornwall, the morning after the liner *Mohegan* hit the Voices Rocks and sank, with the loss of 106 lives, 14 October 1898 *(F.E. Gibson)*

Brigantine *Catherine* and another vessel, stranded on the beach in Seaford Bay, near Newhaven, Sussex, March 1914 *(National Maritime Museum)*

On passage from Freemantle to London, with a cargo of jarrah wood, the three-masted iron barque *Auguste* went ashore at Atherfield, Isle of Wight, 15 February 1900 to become a total wreck *(RLC)*

upon wrecks'; 'John Eastern, master, carrying forces from Ireland to France, has been wrecked at Ilfracombe'; 'Petition of Robert Baden for warrant for all wrecks in west Ireland'; 'Petition of Sir Cloudesley Shovell to the Queen, that by his care and direction, about sixty brass guns were saved out of the prize ships bilged and sunk at Vigo Bay, craves a Royal Bounty'. (It should be noted that four bronze guns of French origin, one or two of which were marked 'Vigo' sometime after the guns were cast, were found on the wreck of the *Association*.) Also amongst such papers can often be found the complete documentation of a wreck, such as the collection of letters from the Collector of Customs at Penzance, to the Treasury Chamber, commencing 23 November 1721. These concern a Dutch ship from Sherrant, bound for Amsterdam, which went ashore near Mullion, in Cornwall, which was seized by the mob, who accidentally set her cargo of brandy on fire. In the blaze, the ship and cargo were destroyed, and two 'wreckers' lost their lives. Diving and salvage, especially in connection with the bullion or specie carried by sunken East Indiamen, occupied the thoughts of many during this particular period. Again, reference to the Treasury State Papers shows: 'A patent by James Trefusis for a diving invention'; 'Captain Jacob Rowe, diving in his engine'; 'Captain Rowe has been on a wreck' (1724); 'John Sydenham is attending an expedition on wrecks' (1724/5); 'Captain Rowe and the Isle of May treasure' (1721); 'Jacob Rowe on board the *Audery* at the Isle of May, has paid the treasury £1,840 as their part of the treasure, to proceed to Sussex and the Lizard' (1722). Rowe was obviously very successful at his profession, as a letter of 30 August 1726 suggests, 'Captain Rowe is diving in the Gulf of Florida, having been fishing on the north coast of Scotland for some weeks, out of which he saved a considerable treasure, said to amount to £25,000' (1728/9). There were of course other divers active at the time; in 1691 a John Williams of Exeter, Devon, was credited with having performed six hours' work, assisted by four other men, at fifteen fathoms. Even as early as 26 April 1622, the

State Colonial Papers reveal that 'the Prince has planned an expedition for the weighing up and recovering of sunken treasure in the East Indies, by means of an engine devised by Cornelius Dryvet, which shall fetch up any weight. Also there is a boat to go under water, where men may live, and if need be, a man may go forth and walk under water twenty or thirty yards and use his arms to any kind of labour'.

A little known Dutch East Indiaman wrecked in the vicinity of Plymouth on or about 21 December 1721, was the *Aaghtekerke* (Nicolaes Rabodus Master). She had sailed from Amsterdam on 16 December, in company with the *Steenhoven* and *Samaritaan*, and was off the Deadman's Head (Dodman Point), when the captain decided to put back for Plymouth. The *Aaghtekerke* anchored, knowing that 'it was dangerous to ride these winter-nights in the Vioers (outer roads of Plymouth), but the cable parted, and she was wrecked close inshore. Next day a great horde of people thronged the shore, waving a flag to show what nation they were, which blew to pieces in the gale. The Collector of Customs at Plymouth wrote to the Treasury, advising them of the plunder of the ship and cargo, suggesting that the persons concerned should be prosecuted. A related incident, since the vessel concerned was a Dutch East India Company man o' war, was the wreck of the forty-four gun *Curacao*, on the east coast of the Isle of Unst, in the Shetlands, north of Scotland, on 9 June 1729. A fleet of East Indiamen returning from Batavia, consisting of eleven ships, under Admiral Gerrit Stocke, was reunited as planned on 9 June off the northern tip of Shetland. A salute of thirteen guns was exchanged with the warships *Curacao* and *Ter Meer, Oranje Galeij, Rosine*, and six provision hookers and galliots, sent to escort them from Shetland to Patria, then they formed convoy and headed south. Dense fog descended, and amongst the deadly rip tides close to Shetland, the *Curacao* struck a rock pinnacle known as Ship Stack and sank. From her crew of 200, a total of 195 were saved and taken aboard the *Ter Meer*, but how the Dutch knew of the incident, when the fog was so thick that the remainder of the fleet was ignorant of the wreck until the *Ter Meer* arrived in Holland with the survivors, remains a mystery.

Less than fifteen miles south of the Ship Stack, and the remains of the *Curacao*, is the island of Fetlar, part of the Shetland group, and the resting place of the twenty-six gun frigate *Wendela*, lost during the night of 18/19 December 1737, with all her crew. Had no salvage been carried out on her during 1738/9, then the remaining cargo would certainly have equalled that of any Spanish 'plate fleet' wreck, such as are found from time to time in the West Indies. On a voyage from Copenhagen to the Danish trading post at Tranquebar, on the coast of Coromandel, the *Wendela* carried '79 bars of silver, 31 sacks of silver coin, sheet metal, pig iron, 1500 bottles of claret, 100 muskets, barrels of wine, rope, copper wire, four tons of coal, grindstones, clothing material, hats, cooking pots, paper, wax, 96 drinking glasses and 37,000 flints'. She belonged to the Danish Asiatic Company, but this was not obvious from the bodies, masts, tackle and fittings which washed ashore on mainland Shetland, and at first a printed book, in Danish, gave the Admiral of Shetland the idea she too, was an East Indiaman. By 13 January 1738, the authorities in the islands had been advised, 'Some money has been saved by such people as could travail down the huge rock where she is wracked,' and shortly after in another letter, 'She has sunk in a very barbarous place. It is very probable if the weather holds good that there will be considerable treasure found here in a short time.' Despite the exclusive legal contract granted by the Admiral to William Irvine to carry out salvage, the gentry and the rabble alike fell on the wreck, and jostled, fought, bribed and stole from all and sundry. Irvine had the distinct advantage of a 'diving engine', almost certainly that of Jacob Rowe, or John Lethbridge, whilst the local lairds, namely Urie, Busta, Symbister, Gloup and Lunna had only grapnels, wrecking tongs, waterglasses, nets and hooks. After two seasons on site, the groups jointly declared having salvaged sixty bars of silver, and twenty-two sacks of coin. But it is unlikely that this was a true account, since even the troops sent to guard the bullion stole some ingots, and hid them in a gulley, although these were recovered.

Holland and Denmark were not the only countries to lose East Indiamen in this part of the British Isles, since the Swedish *Svecia*, a 600-ton merchantman, armed with twenty-eight guns, was also wrecked there in 1740. She had sailed from Bengal that spring, laden with dyewood, saltpetre, silks and cotton, as well as 'iron-bound chests, contents unknown', believed to have been private treasure belonging to her passengers. On the return passage, Chief Officer Diedriech Aget was in command, since out of the 150 individuals aboard when she left Gothenburg in 1739 outward bound, forty had died, including Captain Johan Rattenberg. It was intended that the *Svecia* should pass between Orkney and Fair Isle, but caught by the tide well to the south, between the islands of Ronaldsay and Sanday, she was wrecked on a submerged reef known as the Reefdyke. She remained intact for just three days, during which time it was said that not one islander approached the wreck, which is difficult to believe. It is more likely that this should be interpreted as meaning the islanders would do nothing to save life, being too busy at the age old practice of 'wrecking'. Andrew Monro, the Swedish Company's agent wrote, 'She remaind whole, unparted assunder, for the space of four dayes, yet the inhuman, barbarous inhabitants of that island never gave them the least relief.' Thirty-one individuals escaped to Fair Isle in the ship's boats, thirty left the wreck on a raft, which drifted north never to be seen again, and a further twenty-four left on a second raft, from which only thirteen survived. Shortly after the wreck was abandoned, a gale caused her to break up, disgorging hundreds of bales of cloth ashore, which became entangled with rocks and seaweed for miles. More than 200,000yds of material were salvaged for the owners, but much was secreted or hidden away.

Elsewhere in the British Isles, there were of course countless other shipwrecks, the majority less spectacular, and few rich enough to attract the attention of the crown. The year 1743 is representative of the period, with a reasonably accurate inventory of ship losses available, since Lloyds List, at the time a bi-weekly broadsheet, was by then in its third year of publication. In that year, forty-three wreck incidents were recorded for the entire British Isles, but must be accepted as incomplete, since at the time there was no system of Lloyds agents who, in the nineteenth and twentieth centuries, would report such events direct to London. Two wrecks only were reported in January, the *Martha*, Jamaica to London, lost on the north coast of Scotland, reported on the 10th, and the *John & Hannah*, Riga to Plymouth, lost on Spurn Head, seven days later. February was catastrophic for shipping; due to severe gales, twenty-five vessels were sunk or stranded, the majority between the 24th and 29th of the month. Early in February, the *Hope* was blown ashore near Harwich, and on the 10th, the *St Antonio de Padua* was lost at Lydd, near New Romney. Eleven days later, the *Charming Nancy* off Cape Cornwall, the *Happy Return* in Bigbury Bay, Devon, and the *Maria* in Sandown Bay, Isle of Wight, were added to the toll, although the wool cargo of the latter was saved.

When the north-east gale struck, which caught a great fleet of ships in the Downs by surprise, it lasted for two whole days, over Thursday and Friday, 24/25 February. No less than seventeen ships were wrecked, which included the *Genoa*, London to Gibraltar with victuals, all eight crew drowned; the *Carolina*, and the *Oxford*, both in the same convoy for Gibraltar, the former with four men and a boy lost, the latter with seventeen crew. The *Nottingham*, bound for India; *Charlotte*, in Margate Roads, on passage Carolina to London; *Jennett*, *Mary* and *William & Sarah*, all from London to Carolina; *Crookendon*, London to Barbados; *Industry*, for Virginia; *Globe*, for Dublin and Jamaica; *Recovery*, London to Barnstaple; the *Dolphin*, returning from Gibraltar; *Success*, carrying tobacco, London to Lancaster, and several ships still unidentified. Four days later, another gale caught five ships at anchor at Carnarvon, North Wales, and sank a Dutch dogger, a tobacco-laden brig, and three others. The location of the other losses for that year were confined to those areas already notorious for ship-wrecks, namely Barnstaple Bay, Southwold, the Goodwins, Dublin Bay, Belfast, Beachy Head, Isles of Scilly, Lough Swilly (a whole convoy from Barbados was lost), Padstow and Plymouth.

Of all these, the wreck in the Isles of Scilly was the most valuable, and tragic, since she was an outward bound, treasure laden, VOC ship, and of the 376 persons estimated to have been aboard, all were lost. The first newspaper to print news of the loss was the Amsterdam Dinsdaegse Courant of 23 July 1743, ten days after the incident. Their intelligence came from a Captain Willem Bakker, who passed the *Den Heuvel*, and the *Overnes* outward bound, which should have been accompanied by a third vessel, the *Hollandia*, from which it was deduced that it was the latter which had sunk. The VOC correspondent in London, Gerard Bolwerk, wrote on 24 July that a chest belonging to the *Hollandia*'s first mate, Jan Holst, had been washed ashore, and was the first positive indication that the *Hollandia* was lost. Whether or not the name of the wreck ever appeared in print in England is un-certain. The *London Evening Post* of Tuesday 12 July (old style) broke the news at home, stating: 'By a letter from Penzance we hear that a ship was lately lost off Scilly, and all the crew perished; and that by some papers drove ashore, she appears to be a Dutch East-Indiaman outward-bound.' Final confirmation appeared in the same Dutch newspaper which first printed news of the loss, on 13 August. In a letter dated 2 September, the Heeren Seventeen informed Batavia, 'that the ship Hollandia was lost off the Sorlings on 13 July, "met man en muys"'.

Only two accounts of the wreck exist in this country, one written by Lieutenant Heath in 1750, the other by Parson Troutbeck in 1794, and in neither case is the exact date or name of the ship mentioned. Since Heath was stationed at the

Garrison, on St Marys, to carry out a survey of the islands since May 1744, it is quite remarkable that he appears to have been quite ignorant of these basic details, since his account reads:

About the year 1743 a Dutch East Indiaman outward bound, was lost off St Agnes in about 20 or 22 fathoms of water, with all the people. Their firing of guns, as a signal of the Distress, was heard in the Night; but none could give them assistance. Many of their bodies floated ashore at St Marys and other islands, where they were buried by the Inhabitants. And some were taken up floating on the tide, and were buried. A Dutch Lady, with her children, and Servants, going to her husband, an East-India Governor, was prevented seeing of him by this unhappy Accident. A diver thereupon was sent, by the Dutch Merchants, to discover and weigh the plate of considerable value. But the tide running strong at bottom, and the sea appearing thick, the diver could not see distinctly through the glass of his engine, so returned without success. This wreck remains as a Booty for those who can find it.

The diver employed to find the wreck was John Lethbridge, a man who had already proven his ability, and whose activities were to take him to South Africa, the Cape Verde Islands, the West Indies, and the four corners of the British Isles, but it is reasonable to assume that it was the depth of water that defeated him in the Isles of Scilly. The majority of shipwrecks on which Lethbridge had worked were in less than 35ft, but the *Hollandia* lay in over 100ft, and his 'engine' was not capable of working that deep. The wreck of the *Hollandia*, which had lain undisturbed, an almost unique situation in this depth of water, was finally located on 16 September 1971 by proton magnetometer, and positively identified by diving two days later. Bronze cannon, bearing the monogram of the Amsterdam Chamber of the VOC, narrowed the identification, and silver cutlery bearing the joint arms of the Imhoff and Bentick families, removed all doubt. More than 35,000 silver coins were recovered, including a complete range of artefacts representing life both ashore and afloat in the mid 1700s, and represented a unique collection which unfortunately could not be retained intact. Nine years after its original discovery, excavation is still not complete, and when weather permits, divers are still employed on the seabed to excavate material.

One more Dutch East Indiaman was to be wrecked on the coast of the British Isles before the century reached the half-way mark, and that was the *Amsterdam*. A new vessel of 700 tons and fifty-four guns, she was on her maiden voyage to the East, when Captain Willem Klump finally managed to reach the English Channel after two abortive attempts, leaving Holland on 8 January 1749, but twelve days later was still no further west than Pevensey Bay, where she anchored. In the short time since her original sailing date the previous November, incredible though it may be, fifty of her crew had died from some disease. With another forty men sick and incapable of work, the logic of proceeding further, especially in the depths of winter, was totally inexplicable. On Sunday 26 January, at about three in the afternoon, the vessel's cables parted in the south-west gale and she drifted ashore, watched by almost the entire population of Hastings. By now the majority of the seamen and troops aboard were drunk, having broached the cargo, hence there were insufficient numbers to prevent the looting of the wreck, as literally hundreds swarmed over the bulwarks, stealing cargo, ship's tackle and personal belongings. A company of soldiers were ordered to the scene, who managed to save twenty-seven chests of silver bars, the twenty-eighth having already been broken open, and twenty bars stolen. Although looting continued, it was soon apparent that the *Amsterdam* had settled on a bed of soft clay, and by February she was engulfed to her upper deck, the sea now covering her completely except for low spring tides.

There she remained, broken into from time to time, especially by Irish labourers in the Victorian era, but with only hand tools available and the short time between tides, they saw little profit for their labour. It was not until 1969,

The bridge compass, cover and Flinders Bar, salvaged from the wreck of the steamship *Veritas* of Bergen, which sank off Coverack, Cornwall, on 4 August 1907. Following collision in the Channel and temporary repairs in Portland, she leaked so badly on her way to Wales with pit-props, that she was abandoned to sink. The buoyancy of her timber held her in an almost vertical position, with her bows touching the seabed, for almost two days, before she went under *(RLC)*

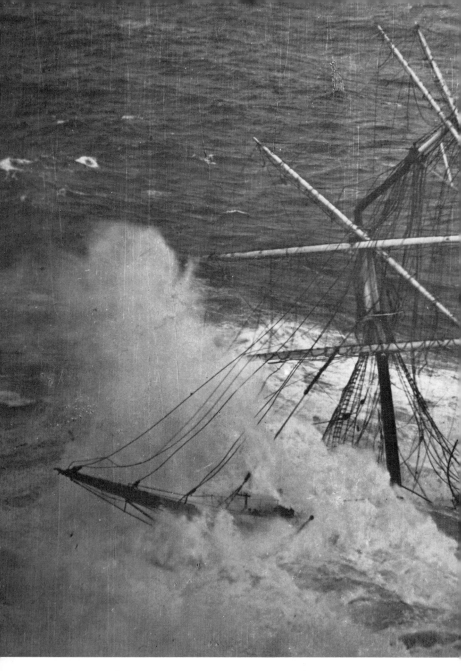

Huge seas slowly pound the once three-masted ship *Cromdale* to pieces, as she lay beneath the coastguard lookout station on the Lizard, Cornwall, May 1913. She came ashore only eighteen days after the *Queen Margaret*, another large sailing vessel was wrecked in the same area *(Hawke Photos)*

Stranded on the Shutter Reef, Lundy Island, North Devon, the battleship HMS *Montagu* struck in fog, and despite tremendous salvage efforts became a total loss, 29 May 1906 *(Naval and Military Record)*

The motor vessel *El Tambo* with 907 head of cattle aboard, caught fire off Strumble Head on 24 February 1977. She was then towed into Fishguard harbour where the fires were extinguished, but she sank at her moorings three weeks later *(Studio Jon Ltd)*

when a mechanical excavator was used on the wreck, that its true potential became obvious, since the first four shovels' full brought up five bronze cannon, a pewter tankard, combs, ivory fans, bottles, wine glasses, candlesticks, brass cartridge holders, shoes, smoothing irons and ship's fittings! The site is now protected under the Historic Wreck Protection Act; meantime, the citizens of Amsterdam are fund raising to have the wreck excavated, and eventually shipped back to its country of origin.

4
GOD SEND THE SHIP IN SAFETY, AMEN

1750–1799

It was ten o'clock at night, when the *Indian Prince* was stranded in dense fog on the coast to the west of Aberthaw, in South Glamorgan, on 30 April 1752. Returning to Bristol from Guinea and St Kitts, she carried a most valuable cargo, consisting of 117 hogsheads of sugar, 35 bags of cotton, 20 tons of ebony wood, one ton of elephants' 'teeth', and several puncheons of rum. The wreck was reported to the Excise officers at both Aberthaw and Barry by noon, the day after the incident, but on arrival, the officials found the entire foreshore swarming with 'country' people. Literally hundreds swarmed over the wreck like ants, who between them had accidentally destroyed or wasted the rum, except for one keg, over which people were fighting. With the incoming tide, the sea washed away most of the bales of cotton, which were lost, and only a small quantity of ivory, Indian goods and ebony were saved. Such scenes at the site of a shipwreck were nothing new, as has already been demonstrated, but on each occasion those in authority continued to express surprise, indignation and dismay, instead of accepting the situation. Throughout this book, the same thing will be seen to have taken place in every corner of the British Isles; even today, the thin veneer we call civilisation will disappear where a wreck is concerned.

The Admiralty have never taken kindly to captains who lose their ships, and for an eighteenth-century officer to survive two courts-martial for such offences, then achieve another command was unusual, if not remarkable, and suggested 'influence' in the right places. Captain Carr Scrope did in fact attend three such courts during his career. At his first it was in the capacity of witness only, which was while serving on board the 2nd-rate *Neptune* in 1744, at which he saw Admiral Mathews, unfairly, dismissed from the service. His first personal trial came as a result of a fire on board the fourteen gun *Whitehaven*, which sank off Ireland, whilst he was her commanding officer during September 1747. He stood before his superiors on 15 October, but was honourably acquitted of 'having caused the loss of His Majesty's man o' war *Whitehaven* through neglect'. Appointed to a sloop on the West Indies station, Scrope was promoted to captain on 14 November 1752, and was then given the 5th-rate, forty-four gun *Assurance*. In late April 1753, the *Assurance*, still commanded by Captain Scrope, was in the Channel and within sight of the Isle of Wight and home. As passengers on board, His Excellency, Governor Trelawney, his wife, and servants, had enjoyed a calm and uneventful crossing from Jamaica, with only a brief call at Lisbon en route. As they approached the Needles which showed stark white in the early morning sunlight, Captain Scrope had two decisions to make: whether to take the short route to Portsmouth west of the Isle of Wight, or the longer, safer one via Spithead; and should he allow his sailing master, David Patterson to take command, or should he assume the responsibility himself? He chose the Needles Channel, with Patterson in charge; had either choice been made differently then the *Assurance* would never have been lost, but as it was, the die was cast. When approached by the Governor and asked, 'How close can we pass to the Needles?', Patterson boasted that they would pass so close, that the ship's ensign at the gaff would actually touch the most westerly rock, on which now stands the Needles lighthouse. Unfortunately, neither the Admiralty, few if any of her captains, and certainly not Patterson were aware that an uncharted rock, now called Goose Rock, lay close to, and west of the Needles, and it was on this that the ship struck, shuddering to a halt, half her bottom planks started. There was no panic on board, since it was broad daylight, early in the day, flat calm, and with only about 25ft of water beneath the keel in which to sink. Attempts were made to pull her off, then she was stripped of her guns, stores and fittings, as well as the cargo of elephants' 'teeth' she carried, and abandoned to the sea as a total loss. No doubt her remains showed above the surface for many a long day, as a reminder to other naval officers that the Needles is no place in which to experiment. Captain Scrope's second court-martial was held on board the sixty-gun *Tiger*, in Portsmouth harbour, on 11 May, before Admiral Boscawen, who acted as President. After hearing the evidence, the captain was acquitted of all blame and discharged from the proceedings, but his unfortunate master, Patterson, went to Marshalsea prison for three months.

That year was a particularly bad one for shipping losses at home, with Lloyds aware of over 120 wrecks, and dozens of others reported too late, or not at all, to be included in the company's weekly lists. During January alone, there were more than two ships lost somewhere in the British Isles every day. In the west country, four ships were stranded at Teignmouth; five wrecked at Prawle Point, and numerous others in Cornwall; while further east, a brandy-laden sloop was lost on Kimmeridge Ledges. At what was then called Brighthelmstone (Brighton), the Dutch vessel *Enegyht*, and a wine laden galliot, the *Young Hendrick*, both for Amsterdam, were wrecked on or about 12 January, and the *Birmingham* four days later. In Ireland, the *Thomas & Rebecca* was 'cast away' off Co Wexford about the 16th; an unidentified West Indiaman in Chewland Bay, near Wexford, about the 19th; the *Lovely Betty* off Kinsale, with most of her crew, on the 23rd; and the *Anne & Margaret* near Waterford. Only one wreck was reported in the north, which was the barque *John & Daniel* lost near Newcastle.

Later the same year, in an accident at the South Dock, Liverpool, on 28 August, the *Maria*, *Elizabeth*, *Frailson*, *Apenride P*, *Frederick*, *Dispatch* and two salt flats were all badly damaged when the dock gates burst open at low water, but no lives were lost. Hazeborough Sands, off Norfolk, claimed three more ships that October: in Scotland, an Irish vessel and the *Alexander & Elizabeth* at Stonehaven, and a Danish ship at Scotenhead, near Peterhead (from which ten carriage guns were recovered), also the *Brockholes* on the eastern side of the Orkneys on 3 October, and the *Prudent Sarah*, 'on a rock' amongst the same islands. From Wales came news that eighty-nine passengers had been drowned when the Newfoundland to Waterford, *William & Mary* of Tynemouth, was lost on Pembrey Sands, five miles west of Llanelly, on 15 November. On Anglesey, the *Thomas Hill* went down off Holyhead, and the *Fortuna* in Carnarvon Bay. Of the many wrecks denied an entry in Lloyds List, the *Vainiver* (Master John Maffin), from Dieppe, is typical. Details of her loss near Newton, a coastal village near Swansea in South Wales, appeared in the *Kentish Post & Canterbury News Letter* of 29 December, of all places! On passage from Lisbon to 'Harve de Grace', her cargo of 850 chests of China oranges, 14 chests of lemons, 650 frails (rush-baskets) of figs, and 84 planks of Brazilian mahogany caught the attention of the 'wreckers', who removed anything capable of being carried.

The degree of documentation associated with a wreck, even in the 1700s was extensive, consequently a bundle of such papers in the Devon Records Office relating to the wreck of a Dutch ship in Bigbury Bay, on 10 January 1753, which includes letters, inventories, declarations and affidavits, is of particular interest. Lloyds List No 1786, of 12 January, records only 'an unidentified galliot hoy, stranded in Bigbury Bay, cargo of wine and brandy, from Cherante to Hamburg'; whereas a letter from George Taylor, written at Totnes, Devon, on 16 January gives a much better appreciation of the incident:

> I'm to acquaint you that last Wednesday night about ten, a Hamburg Dutch galliot burthen about 100 tons, loaded with wine, brandy, coffee, indigo and bales of saffron, bound from

Zant to Hamburg, was stranded on Thurlestone Sands within the premises of your Royalty. Thursday morning I went thither to do what lay in my power to prevent ye Country from plundering her and to save ye cargo and have ye pleasure to let your honour know that more than three parts of four is saved ... the Customs officers of Plymouth, Dartmouth and Salcome all assisted in saving ye goods ... ye cargo is valued at about £3000, and a great part of ye goods are saved. Saturday evening there was come not less than 10000 people who came from remote parts in order to plunder ye cargo, which they had certainly done if ye Plymouth official had not ordered a party of soldiers to attend ... by accident one of ye ring leaders was killed, his being drunk and fell upon one of ye soldiers bayonets fixt on ye gun ... more goods have been saved out of this vessel than all ye ships that have been stranded for fifty years past.

By comparison, the following year was a lean one for those who made their living from wrecks, since less than forty incidents are recorded, for one of which the Lizard lighthouse keeper was responsible. Following earlier complaints concerning the short distances over which the light could be seen, the Trinity Brethren erected a second tower, so that the two fires were orientated 'W5°N, and E5°S, with a distance of seventy-two yards between', and was first used on 22 August 1752. During the night of 21 December 1754 neither light was showing, and as a consequence, the snow *Friendship*, Master Bishop, from Jamaica to London, was wrecked on the outer rocks, and lost with all hands.

It was a November gale in 1756, that put the Dutch ship *Jonge Hendrick*, ashore at Sormills, Dartmouth. In a relatively sheltered location, salvage was possible immediately, and by the time the owner's agent arrived in Devon, there was an impressive pile of goods and ship's stores in a local warehouse. But nothing could be removed from the site until the legal processes of law had been satisfied, and these can take a long time. First, the Crown had to be satisfied that the goods had a rightful owner, and that they were not unclaimed wreck. This necessitated receipt of proof that the items salvaged had in fact been shipped from Leghorn in the first place, and since the originals would not have been in English, then an English translated version was required, one example of which read:

Leghorn 10 September 1756

Shipped by the Grace of God, in good order, at this Port of Leghorn, by Jacob Maria Nataling, a Tuscan subject for his proper account, in and upon the ship called the Young Henry, Captain Jurian Ahrens of Holland, to conduct and consign in this his present voyage to Amsterdam to Messrs Thomas and Adrian Hope or to their assigns, the goods at foot named and numerated, dry and whole and well conditioned, markt as per margin and thus said captain promises to consign the same at his safe arrival, and for freight it shall be paid him twenty five current florins in all, with 10 per cent average Flat money, in witness whereof this Bill of Lairngwith with others of ye same form shall be signed by said captain, and he not being able to write, a third person for him, and the one of which Bills being accomplished, the other to stand of no value, and so God send the ship in Safety, Amen.

SW			
S	2	We declare two chests containing two tables of Marble	
$\frac{4}{N\ 4}$	2	Do the same	Do small, containing two pictures of
		The whole extremely well conditioned.	

Signed Contents unknown
Jurian Harints

The list prepared by the Dartmouth Customs officials of goods salvaged from the *Jonge Hendrick* is surprisingly comprehensive, and must have represented a far greater percentage of the cargo and ship's fittings than an owner would ever expect. Divided into three sections, it reads:

Effects saved att Sormills December 1756 belonging to the Dutch ship called the Jonge Hendrick—Juryen Agents and Master and cargo, stranded there in her voyage from Leghorne to Cadiz and Amsterdam—viz:

Ships Materials Etc

		1 Best Bower
4 Anchors	—	2 Common
		1 Kedge
8 Guns	—	6 Carriage
		2 Swivell

The owners are Messrs Pieter de Vriese Claas Zoon, marchants att Amsterdam.

1 Muskett Barrell
26 Junks of cable
1 small coil of rope, about 12 fathom
1 piece of sail and one block
1 piece of ye foremast—about 15ft
1 iron tiller
1 handscrew
1 ships bell sound and good
1 lead pump 20ft long
1 Pewter tea kettle
1 Hanger

Cargo
Marble — 589 Floor stones   373 whole
                                     216 broken

2 polished slabs 6ft long in a Case
12 pieces polished marble in a Case. Two
    pieces broken.
4 Statues
1 small block in a chest
4 chimney pieces—parts only
1 piece of painting of ye
    Imperial Family of
    Germany
1 case of Aloes about 3

Not claimed yet by anybody

Owners Messrs Abrm. Van Notten

Owners Messrs Muilman & Son Amsterdam

Wearing Apparrel

1 Grego cloak	1 Coate Dark silk
1 Great Coate	1 Wastecoate Camblett
1 Light Great Coate	1 white frock and 4
1 Cotton Wastecoate	chequed shirts
& 2 old Ruggs	1 pair striped drawers
1 old Fustain	& 2 Wiggs
Wastecoate	

Supposed to belong to the sailors.

Following a shift of her cargo when 20 miles south-east of Great Yarmouth, the coaster *Sea Rhine* sent out a Mayday signal on 11 February 1975. She later rolled over and sank, but not before the Gorleston lifeboat *Khami* had rescued her five-man crew (*H.E. Appleton. Gorleston RNLI*)

Following collision between the 493-ton MV *Biscaya* and a French tug, some 42 miles off Lowestoft on 13 December 1974, a dramatic rescue of the coaster's crew was carried out by the Gorleston lifeboat. In these remarkable photographs, the *Biscaya* is shown slowly foundering 34 miles east of the Outer Gabbard lightship (*H.E. Appleton. Gorleston RNLI*)

Five months later, in April the following year, a Charles Hope Weir was writing from Edinburgh, to enquire as to the whereabouts of his luggage, carried by the wrecked vessel, in which there were some valuable paintings:

Note of Goods Ship'd on Board the young Hendrick by Sigm. Batti and consigned by Messrs. Willis and Panton to Messrs. Hope att Amsterdam from Leghorn

H. No. 1. A Trunk with Cloaths Books etc.
No. 2. A Box of Pictures containing 5 Portraits, small, with Frames and Glasses done in Crayons.
A Gentleman's Portrait done in Oil Colours,
Another, being a Copy of the same
A Family Piece, done from Guido being a Susanna and the Two Elders
A Small Picture from Carach, being a David with Goliath's head
A Little Box with a Venus in Ivory.

Stephen Penny of Dartmouth, who appears to have been personally involved in the salvage work (although he appears from his handwriting to have been a gentleman), was complaining over two years later that he had still not received satisfaction. In his letter of 10 December 1758, he writes:

It is now two years since I first applied to Sir William Courtenay in relation to ye stranded Effects at Sormills. About a year ago (I believe it is) he was pleased to refer me to his Steward, Mr Ley at Exeter, and now in a letter today from Mr Ley I am referred to you, wherein he tells me (tho' never mentioned one Syllable of it in any one of his letters before), that if I had produced to you authentic evidence to whom ye goods belonged with proper papers from ye owners, they would have been delivered up long ago, on paying ye.

The fear of being trapped below decks in a shipwreck must have been a nightmare among a great many men in the age of sail—the more so if those men were handcuffed and in a battened-down hold. This was the situation in which some seventy unfortunate individuals found themselves on 28 November 1760, while aboard the Admiralty hired tender *Caesar*. She had lain at anchor in Mumbles Roads, near Swansea, in company with the *Reeves*, while groups of seamen and officers from both vessels went ashore as 'press-gangs'. Having 'recruited' a number of men by the simple expedient of knocking them unconscious and carrying them aboard, both ships weighed anchor and sailed for Plymouth. Part way down the Bristol Channel, the change of tide and unfavourable weather compelled them to return to anchor. In fading light, those aboard the *Caesar* mistook Pwll du Head for Mumbles, and in anticipation of gently shoaling water, the deep approach to the former was unexpected, and they were ashore before the leadsman's line indicated danger. Driven by the heavy seas between two huge rocks she remained fast, with water pouring in below the waterline.

An unknown number of survivors, including Captain Adam Drake and his lieutenant, reached shore by climbing over the bowsprit onto the rocks, and scaling the cliff face at High Pennard. Next day the shore was strewn with the bodies of the 'pressed' men, who had drowned like rats in a trap. Local tradition suggests that ninety persons were buried on 29 November, the day after the wreck, and seven the next—all in a common grave at a place now called Gravesend, on the eastern slopes of the headland. Lloyds List for 5 December (No 2598), however, reports only sixty-three men and three women. Since she was only on hire to the navy, and not an Admiralty vessel, there was no court-martial. But the fact that she was on hire explains why such a large assortment of weapons, including 44 muskets, 27 pistols, 50 swords, etc, were salvaged, and why, that September, George Knight of Swansea sent to Bristol 'eight guns saved from the *Ceezur*'. By coincidence, there were two other vessels of the same name wrecked in the British Isles during 1760, one near Plymouth, reported as 'lost' on 19 February, the other on Deal beach, in the Downs, during early December.

The year 1760 was a particularly unfortunate one for the navy, which lost an eighty-two-gun 2nd-rate; a seventy-gun 3rd-rate; a fourteen-gun sloop, and a small vessel stranded and badly damaged. In books concerning the history of North Wales and Anglesey, there are several references to a fourteen-gun frigate, the *Ann*, wrecked at Dinas Dinlle in Caernarvon Bay on 3 November 1760, with eighteen men lost from a crew of thirty-seven. A quotation from Captain Seth Houghton's report is said to state:

> Accordingly we bore away and passed Caernarvon Bar, which probably might have been attempted had we not seen the *Pearl*, a Liverpool ship, ashore there where all the crew perished. Our ship struck a little after two in the afternoon about two miles to leeward of the Bar, and a quarter mile from shore. Some of the people partly by the boat, and partly by swimming, immediately got on shore, but I continued on board till near five, to persuade the remainder to attempt their own preservation. However, as they seemed obstinately determined in their resolution of continuing on board, I then took leave of them and leapt off the weather forechains with my cork jacket.

It is interesting to look more closely at this incident, since it is typical of the apparent anomalies which exist in the history of shipwreck. The navy has never owned a vessel larger than a hired cutter of twelve guns named *Ann*, and certainly never a frigate, which by definition would have been armed with at least forty guns, and carried 200 crew or more. Even thirty-seven men would have been insufficient to man the fourteen muzzle-loading cannon carried by HMS *Ann*, so the incident remains something of a mystery. Certainly, the loss of the *Pearl* is authentic, since it is on record that she was lost with all hands, including Captain Pollard, whilst returning to Liverpool from South Carolina. More fortunate than either of these two craft, the *Royal Escape* went ashore on the beach at Deal, Kent, on 6 January, during a gale; but after unloading she was warped off and saved. Built as the fourteen-gun yacht *Surprise*, 34 tons, before conversion to a transport vessel in 1736, she had been used for the escape of the future King Charles II after the Battle of Worcester, from which it derived its unusual name.

The *Ramillies* (ex-*Royal Katherine*, ex-*Katherine*), apart from the tragic loss of life associated with her stranding, may not have been too great a loss to the navy, since she was an incredible ninety-six years old when she was blown ashore at Bolt Tail near Salcombe, Devon. A ninety-two gun, 2nd-rate, of over 1,500 tons, she had given distinguished service in almost every major naval action over the past century, and was on Channel blockade duty against the French when lost on 15 February 1760. In bad weather her captain mistook Burgh Island, in Bigbury Bay, for Looe Island, and made to the east thinking he was heading for Plymouth Sound only to find his ship embayed. After parting several cables he drove ashore. Over 700 died in that wreck, Midshipman Harrold being the only commissioned officer to survive. On or about the same day, the fourteen-gun naval sloop *Eagle* (reported at the time as being a frigate) was lost in King Road, off the River Avon, whilst on passage from Bristol to London. By contrast, it was not storm but sheer negligence which caused the seventy-gun *Conqueror* to become a total wreck in Plymouth Sound. She stranded on the extreme south-east corner of St Nicholas Isle on 26 October the same year, as a direct result of pilot error. At a court-martial held aboard the *Barfleur*, he was found 'highly blameable in getting the ship underway in such weather as prevailed at the time, and from his want of knowledge as a seaman, did not direct the proper sails to be set, by which neglect the *Conqueror* drove to leeward and was stranded'. Henry Harris, the unfortunate man responsible, spent eighteen months in Marshalsea prison as a result.

Although there were to be no more major naval accidents until the mid 1770s, there was no shortage of 'ordinary' shipwrecks. On 15 February 1763 a Berwick newspaper commented: 'The shores of the neighbourhood are strewed with wrecks and dead bodies, the effects of the late storms.'

Gales in the following October stranded three ships between Shields and Blyth, wrecked three others at Sunderland, two in Robin Hood's Bay, one at Berwick, and a further two at Redcar. There is seldom any humour in such incidents, but that of 12 November 1764, concerning the *Beulah*, Captain Green, New York to London, proved the exception. Forced into the Bristol Channel by storm, and stranded near Barnstaple on the North Devon coast, the Tide Surveyor for the town was looking after the wreck to prevent looting, when a bureau or chest of drawers washed ashore. He was about to examine the contents, when the wife of Richard Budd, the tenant of the land upon which the vessel was lying, approached him in what he later described as 'a most outrageous manner'. She then proceeded to hit him over the head with an iron ladle, claiming that whatever was cast ashore here was her husband's property; the ancient 'Right of Wreck' asserting itself again. Eventually, after chasing the poor man up and down the beach several times, belabouring him till he was quite badly injured, some boatmen caught her and held her down, while the 'officer persevered in his duties'. In the drawers of the piece of furniture all that was found was three silver teaspoons, a silver candlestick and some old gold lace from a uniform jacket.

Two classic 'wrecking' incidents illustrate the difficulties facing the authorities if immediate steps were not taken to prevent plunder of a ship ashore. An *Exeter Flying Post* newspaper account in 1771 reports on the loss of a brig:

St Peter, William Causey master, from London laden with groceries from this city, having overshot her port and got opposite Torkay on Friday night last (1 September) in a heavy gale of wind to the eastward. She drove ashore about a mile to the westward of Tor Abbey and was dashed to pieces. The cargo is supposed to be worth £4000, the greater part of which has since been lost, the crew being happily saved. Immediately on going to pieces, the country people came down in great numbers to plunder the wreck, and even robbed the captain of his watch, on which George Cary esq of Tor Abbey, accompanied by his brother and several armed men, secured the ring leaders whom they sent immediately on board of a man o' war, and by their endeavours saved all they could of the cargo and *secured it in their cellars.*

Unfortunately we are not told for whose benefit it was thus put under lock and key, since the old traditions were still prevalent, and persisted for a long time to come.

The second incident is of particular importance. It concerns a wreck in Anglesey and some of its well-to-do inhabitants of 1773, and may be one of the very few authenticated instances where 'false-lights' were displayed. Much has been written on this subject, and while popularly cherished as an alleged activity particularly of west-countrymen in Devon and Cornwall, there is little hard evidence to prove it actually took place. The account, contained in the *Annual Register* for that year, could well be worth research in greater depth, since one or more of the miscreants appeared before a local magistrate at an island court. The account reads:

At the Assize, bills of indictment preferred by Captain Chilcot, late of the *Charming Jenny*, against three opulent inhabitants of the isle of Anglesea, one of whom is possessed of a considerable estate and has been offered £5000 bail, in order to be free until the next assize when he will be charged with piracy. On 11 September 1773, in bad weather and *in consequence of false lights being discovered,* where the captain bore for shore, where the vessel valued at £19,000 went to pieces and all the crew, except captain and wife perished, who were brought ashore by the sea on a piece of wreck. The wreckers found them exhausted on the beach; they cut the buckles from his shoes, and deprived him of every stitch of covering. Happy to even be left alive, he hastened to the waters edge to find his wife where her half-naked and plundered corpse presented itself to his view. The captains wife unfortunately had (carried) two bank rolls of considerable value with her, and seventy guineas in her pocket, Five men are concerned.

The vessel may well have been part of a small convoy from the West Indies to Liverpool, since the *Will* and the *Edward* were both lost near Holyhead at the same time.

In 1774 the toll of naval ships was increased by a further

two. Had not the 6th-rate *Cerberus* been saved after going ashore on Penlee Point, when leaving Plymouth Sound as part of Sir James Douglas's fleet, the total could well have been three. Within the Sound, the frigate *Torbay* caught fire and burnt to the water's edge, whilst the seventy-four-gun *Kent* blew up. Whilst firing the time-honoured salute to her Admiral, sparks were blown inboard by the wind and fell into an open ammunition chest, in which there was loose powder. There was a violent explosion. This forced up the deck beams of the entire quarterdeck, blew off all the deck planking, and killed or seriously wounded fifty crew. A drummer boy, said to be sitting by the chest, was blown clean through the sky-light, to fall uninjured into the sea.

A merchantman wrecked that year was the *Elizabeth*, Captain Weeks, Bristol to Cork and Jamaica, which stranded on a rock named St Dunnel's, on the Welsh coast, and went to pieces. Of her thirty-seven passengers and crew only eleven were saved. Captain Sackville of the 33rd Regiment, one of the passengers aboard, was found dead on the foreshore with his arms locked tightly around the corpse of his wife. They were so fixed in that position that they were buried undisturbed, in a special double coffin. Meanwhile, at the entrance to Fowey harbour in Cornwall, the Dutch *Jaff Johanna Christina* became another total loss due to storm. The Lord of the Manor of Menabilly, the seat of the Rashleighs, kept his men busy collecting '137 elephants teeth of 30/50lbs each, iron hoops, brandy, lead, a broken bilge pump, an old blunderbuss, three cannon, three cutlasses and a pistol iron'—the sum total of salvage.

In the June of 1774, the unfortunate Mr Day met his death in the second of his submarine 'experiments' which enjoyed a greater alliance to wagering than to science. Earlier in the year, he had been submerged in a sealed vessel in the relatively sheltered waters of the Cattewater, Plymouth, for twelve hours. He then unscrewed the bolts holding the false bottom and ballast in place, and rose to the surface, to collect the many bets he had accepted. He announced he would repeat the 'experiment' in 132ft, off the Hoe. To this end he persuaded a London backer to purchase and convert a 50-ton brig, the *Maria*. In her hold a chamber-like box was constructed, with a counter-balanced sealed hatch, which could be secured from inside by chains. Four huge bolts, passing through lead pipes in the keel, held back 20 tons of stone ballast blocks, which could be jettisoned as required. At 2 pm on 20 June, Mr Day was sealed inside, along with a hammock, watch, wax taper, flint, bottle of water and two ship's biscuits, after which the vessel was towed to a position midway between Firestone Point and St Nicholas Isle. The flooding bungs were removed and the craft filled, but refused to sink, and so haphazard were the calculations regarding buoyancy, that it took a further 20 tons of ballast to put it under. Needless to say, neither the vessel nor Mr Day was ever seen again, and as a local newspaper stated so beautifully but sadly, 'Mr Day descended into perpetual night.' Many were the theories on what had gone wrong: 'The change in temperature of the air within the chamber rendered it an almost perfect vacuum', was one suggestion. Another decided 'that the pressure does not depend on the depth but on the coldness peculiar to such a depth. His blood must have been chilled into an immediate coagulation.' So much for eighteenth-century understanding of basic physics.

The last quarter of the century saw a proliferation of wrecks, several of which were of considerable importance. On 14 November 1779, the homeward-bound English East India Company vessel *Valentine*, from Madras via St Helena, in company with seven other ships, struck a reef known as Le Neste, at the western end of Brecqhou, a small islet in the Channel Isles, and went to pieces.

Another wreck is possibly remembered more for the subsequent diving activities on the wreck in the first rigid helmet apparatus, than for the unfortunate loss of Admiral Kempenfelt and some 900 others. This was the capsize and sinking of the *Royal George* in the Solent, near Portsmouth on 28 August 1782, which ranks as one of the great disasters of the century.

Inquest jury and other officials of the court visiting the salvaged stern section of the paddle-steamer *Princess Alice*, which was run down in Barking Reach, River Thames, 3 September 1878 *(Illustrated London News)*

The visit of the Prince of Wales, to the wreck of HMS *Eurydice*, a naval sail training ship for boy seamen, which capsized in a squall in Sandown Bay, Isle of Wight, 24 March 1878 *(Illustrated London News)*

The French trawler *Laverenne* abandoned under the high cliffs of Land's End. She went aground in fog in September 1972, and in less than ten days was completely demolished by the sea *(Eric Collins collection)*

The Aberdeen trawler *Nevena*, stranded on the north-west corner of Copinsay, an island with a population of seven, off Orkney in Scotland, on 6 December 1973 *(Eric Collins collection)*

The French steamer *Maurice Bernard* on the rocks at Kennack Sands, near the Lizard, on 25 May 1925. She went ashore almost on top of the remains of the *Normand*, a small steamer wrecked on 2 April 1914, and close to the point where the *Viola* stranded three years before *(F.E. Gibson)*

Preparing to depart with a fleet to relieve besieged Gibraltar, the 100-gun, 1st-rate man o' war required a last-minute repair to a below-water fitting which was leaking. To bring the affected area above the surface, it was necessary to heel the ship to port, by taking guns from one side to the midship's line. But, old and overladen, some internal part of her fabric gave way under the strain. 'She gave a great jerk or crack first, and within a moment after another, and went down, and I jumped out of the starboard stern port.' So testified John Smart, gunner's yeoman, at the subsequent court-martial. That her structure was rotten was in no doubt, since after she had been docked that summer for inspection, Vice Admiral Milbank reported: 'I found her so bad, that I do not recollect there was a sound timber in the open. The officers of the yard said they should be able to make her last a summer.' Fifty years later, extensive diving operations in clearing the wreck were conducted by John and Charles Deane, inventors of the 'standard' or 'rigid' helmet diving apparatus.

Five years after the *Valentine* was lost in the Channel Isles, the Company suffered another financial blow when the *Halsewell*, outward-bound for Bengal, ended her days on the rocks at Peverel Point, St Albans Head, some ten miles east of Portland Bill. She left London between Christmas and New Year 1785, with 240 persons aboard, of whom 166 were dead before the week was out. Caught on a lee shore by a southerly gale and successively losing all her anchors, she went ashore about 3 am on 16 January. Her captain, his two daughters, three mates, eight passengers and some 160 crew and soldiers drowned in the incident, the cause of which was attributed to 'the want of subordination in the crew, as while there was a probability of saving her, the seamen absolutely refused to obey the officers, and on being threatened with chastisement, exultingly answered in the laconic manner, saying "You be damned, if you dare damn my eyes, but I'll Loughborough you", alluding to a late verdict in the Court of Common Pleas.' An East India pilot yacht was sent to work on the wreck, the value of the vessel and cargo being estimated at £70,000. Among the cargo was a 'most curious and valuable assortment of fire arms, and several founts of printing type, there was much plunder of the dead bodies'. The same report mentions that not far from where the *Halsewell* foundered, a man o' war was lost some twenty years earlier, and that in the same gale that wrecked the East Indiaman, eleven Swedish merchantmen were lost on the Essex coast in one night.

The last decade of the century saw four more naval disasters, over a thousand dead lying on the beaches around Portland, an historic wreck find in Ireland, and other losses. Underwater exploration in the twentieth century has brought hundreds of old wreck sites to the attention of the public, but in eighteenth-century Ireland was a totally unexpected occurrence. Early in 1793, the remains of a large wreck were discovered near Rutland harbour, Co Donegal, only 3ft beneath the surface at low water. Four massive cannon of bronze were recovered, which from their markings were thought to be from some Armada vessel, wrecked over 200 years earlier. Severe gales over an eight-day period in November 1795 caused phenomenal damage and loss of life. The first victims were six transport ships blown ashore in the Cattewater at Plymouth over 18/19 November. On Portland beach, Dorset, the *Golden Grove*, London to St Kitts and five transports, the *Piedmont*, *William Pitt*, *Catharina*, *Venus* and *Thomas*, all carrying troops and ordnance, were wrecked with no more than a score of survivors between them. Inhabitants of Brighton awoke on the 19th of that month to find two vessels smashed to pieces on the beach; and near Portsmouth, the *Briton*, *Gloria*, *Princess Maria Carolina*, *Commerce* and *Britannia*, all ended their days in the shallows. Only in Dorset were there reports of heavy loss of life, and there newspapers spoke of 'the foreshore littered with broken ships and corpses, —over a thousand dead to be taken care of by the parish—there is much looting and pillage of the dead.' At the same time, information was received on the mainland of the wreck of a Dutch East Indiaman in the Isles of Scilly, on or about 14

October. Details of the loss were given in a private letter which read:

> I have a moment allowed me to inform you that one of the Dutch East Indiamen, a prize to the *Sceptre*, a large china ship which left the Shannon last Friday under convoy, was yesterday morning at 3 o'clock totally lost and gone to pieces, having struck the most western rocks of the Isles. The accident is said to have been wholly occassioned by the obstinaccy of the person on board having the command, said to be the Mate, who was appraised by those on board of the immediate danger, told what the light was and that land and breakers were run ahead. He is himself drowned, said to having jumped overboard as soon as the ship struck. About twenty-four others are lost and forty-five saved, who were taken on board Sir Edward Pellew's ship, which with the *Quebec* and *La Resolution* frigates, were lying in the Road, waiting to be joined by the *Cestene*. The Dutch East Indiaman is laden chiefly with tea and china, which is all gone to the bottom, the cargo being valued at £140,000.

The following year, 1796, saw three incidents of some importance, commencing with the English East Indiaman *Dutton*, which was on passage for the West Indies with part of the Queen's 2nd Regiment aboard. She struck Mount Batten Shoal on entering Plymouth Sound, the warning buoy having blown away in a gale. Minus her rudder, she was swept helpless on to the rocks beneath the Hoe on 28 January, watched by thousands on the shore, who did nothing to assist. Panic broke out on board when all three masts fell, only minutes after she struck—whereupon the ship's officers abandoned the vessel, and only the exertions and leadership of Sir Edward Pellew, a naval captain who witnessed the wreck from ashore, saved the lives of all 600 left aboard. Three weeks later, the foreshore at Porthleven (40 miles to the west, in Cornwall, commonly known as Loe Bar) was strewn with the corpses and belongings of almost 600 troops from a Dragoon Regiment, on board a transport forming part of Admiral Christian's convoy, wrecked on 17 February. The third incident was the blowing-up of the thirty-two gun *Amphion*, in the Hamoaze, opposite the area now occupied by Devonport Dockyard. It was late in the afternoon of 22 September, a fine summer's day; a traditional farewell party was in progress on board, given for the relatives and friends of the ship's company. Contemporary accounts of the accident suggest that guests and crew numbered some 312 persons, of whom ten men, one woman and a child survived the blast. Without warning, a massive explosion at 4.30 pm ripped through the ship, causing the entire forepart to disintegrate, the remainder sinking instantly in 10 fathoms. As with previous explosions, theft of gunpowder or carelessness was the assumed cause. A similar verdict was expressed when the French prize frigate *La Coquille* blew up at the foot of Millbrook Lake, in Plymouth's Cattewater, just before Christmas Day. The flames set the coal-laden brig *Endeavour* on fire, and both burnt to the waterline and sank.

It was during the late autumn of 1970, that a chance find by a diver in the Isles of Scilly revealed the resting place of the Scarborough-built barque *Juno*. Research by the finders revealed that the name had disappeared from Lloyds Register after 1784, and it was a reasonable assumption that she had been lost that year. The *Juno* was a transport vessel, on passage from London to either Jamaica or Barbados, and was reported in London as being lost on 10 January 1797, and therefore the incident must have taken place around the 5th. More interesting still was the fact that the *Juno* was not alone the night she sank, since the same source shows that the brig *Albion*, of 104 tons, ten crew, Captain Johnson, Ipswich to Bristol, was lost at the same time and place. As to why the *Juno* disappeared from Lloyds Register to sink thirteen years later, suggests that she changed both ownership and nationality, and hence became registered outside of the British Isles.

As the 1700s came to an end, three more men o' war were lost, the *Colossus* in the Isles of Scilly; *Nautilus* on the Yorkshire coast, and the *Weazle* in the Bristol Channel (or, more accurately, on the coast of North Devon). *Colossus* was a 3rd-rate, seventy-four-gun warship, built in 1787, which had suffered the ravages of sun and worm in the Mediterranean for two years without any major refitting. By November 1798, she was fit for little else than to escort a convoy back to England, which arrived in Scilly on 7 December. Three days later, *Colossus* was caught at anchor in a south-east gale, and at 8 pm on 10 December, struck the rocks of Southward Well, just south of Samson island, and filled. With only one casualty (a quartermaster who drowned when he fell overboard), the wreck may appear to be of little significance except that she carried in her hold part of Sir William Hamilton's personal collection of antiques. Few people can be unaware of the discovery of thousands of pottery shards, pieces of once priceless Etruscan vases and the like, that have been salvaged from the site over three years, and painstakingly classified, cleaned and reconstructed where possible by the British Museum. The same evening that the *Colossus* was lost, a French privateer brig, of fourteen guns was driven in to Scilly by the gale, struck a rock and sank in deep water with all hands. This wreck has never been identified, and still awaits location.

Two months after *Colossus* was struck from the register of fighting ships, near blizzard conditions put the naval sloop *Nautilus* ashore on 2 February 1709, near the King and Queen rocks, in Filey Bay, Yorkshire. That same month, another sloop o' war, the *Weazle*, sank on Baggy Point on 12 February, on the north coast of Devon. Her total complement is uncertain, but with a funeral service for 106 persons at Northam church, others laid to rest at Braunton and Georgeham, it would appear few if any of her crew escaped. So ended a century filled with tragic shipwrecks, and an absolutely appalling loss of life, especially amongst the men o' war, which fortunately was never to be repeated. Seamen of the period were still unaware of the immense changes that lay less than twenty-five years ahead. Soon iron and steel would replace timber, and rudimentary steam engines the need for sail; changes which brought about a whole new generation of problems, and an even greater number of ship losses.

5

THE COMING OF STEAM
1800–1849

The degree of change to which seafarers and ship owners of the nineteenth century were to be subjected, could not possibly have been forecast. At the turn of the eighteenth century, merchantmen and men o' war alike were still being built, crewed and handled, in much the same manner as they had been 200 years previously. Merchant ships were operated as the owners or masters saw fit, being allowed to carry as much cargo as they cared to put in the holds; to show whatever lights they chose, although common practice had established a degree of international practice; to carry lifeboats or lifebelts, or not bother; to show such a wide range of 'distress' signals that no-one who saw them was ever really sure help was required; and to act in the proximity of other ships as each captain thought best. These anomalies in behaviour, the amount of food a seaman should be given, when and how he should be paid, the space allocated him for sleep, the navigational ability of his superiors, lights, signals, loading, bedding, fire precautions, and a thousand other details were to be laid down in the form of a Merchant Shipping Act before the 1800s were over. Ship building was to see the introduction of iron in place of timber, steam engines instead of sail, and wire for rope. Ashore, two line-throwing apparatus inventions greatly reduced the loss of life among shipwrecks, as did the introduction of professional lifeboats, capable of going to sea in all weathers. These and other changes must have been as revolutionary in the 1800s, as the electronic silicon chip is today. Possibly the Merchant Shipping Act of 1854 had more effect on the everyday life of seamen than any other single event in the history of the sea. Born out of the Shipwreck Committee, which sat for the best part of five years investigating every aspect of how and why ships were lost, the Act was responsible for reducing the phenomenal loss of lives and wrecks which peaked around 1860/65. It also established safety standards which were eventually adopted by every maritime nation in the world.

The new century was barely hours old when the ship *Ajax* parted from her cables in Sunderland Roads and grounded near the Bar at low water. As the tide turned, with twelve keels of coal in her hold, so she began to beat the bottom, until it appeared she must go to pieces any moment. Her master and some of the crew took to the rigging, but expecting her masts to fall any moment. The remainder of the seamen clung to deck fittings, to avoid being swept away by the huge breakers that swept the length of the deck. Shortly after, the *Ajax* fell on her side, and began to break up, whereupon the cobles which had been awaiting an opportunity to rescue the crew dashed in, and saved all but one seaman. A messenger had been sent off some time earlier to fetch the Shields lifeboat, but there is no record of it attending this wreck. The inhabitants of Sunderland and Wearmouth set about collecting subscriptions for the men who had saved the crew, with some extra money going to the widow of the drowned man. A total of 158gns was shared out amongst the local boatmen, a quite incredible amount of money considering that shipwrecks were frequent in the area. Unfortunately, no such assistance was extended to the relatives of the sailors lost in the wreck of the West Indiaman *Active*, sunk half a mile from Margate pier on 10 January 1803. Bound for Greenock with 300 hogsheads of sugar in her hold, the 350-ton vessel, a new ship, lost nine of her nineteen crew. *The Times* of 20 January reported the captain's thanks 'to the Marchioness of Hertford and the Ladies and Gentlemen of Margate, for their kind and liberal assistance given them', each man having been given a change of clothing, and a hot dinner.

Although the heavy loss of men o' war in the 1700s was never to be repeated, there were of course incidents. Only a few days after the *Ajax* was lost, HM gunboat No 35, the *Mastiff*, carrying 2 × 32 pounder, and 10 × 18 pounder carronades was wrecked on Cockle Sands, in Yarmouth Roads, Norfolk, with a heavy loss of life. By way of contrast, the massive seventy-four-gun *Venerable* became a total wreck in Torbay, with only three casualties. Renewal of the war against France saw the Brest fleet, under the command of Cornwallis, once again in Torbay, and this resulted in a most unfortunate accident at Goodrington. Brought about by a seaman who fell overboard, it may well be the only occasion in which a major warship has been lost as a direct result of such a simple accident. After bringing the fleet to anchor on 23 November 1804, the Admiral signalled an immediate and totally unexpected departure the following day, but could hardly have chosen a more inopportune time. The order was passed just before 5 pm, by which time the various ship's captains had naturally assumed they would remain at anchor all night. They had hence ordered stoppers passed, and cables frapped to prevent chafing, detailed anchor watches and sent the remainder of the hands below for supper. To expect a large fleet of sailing ships to weigh anchor and leave Torbay in the dark was courting disaster, which is exactly what happened. On board the *Venerable*, Captain John Hunter waited impatiently for word from the forecastle that the anchor and cable were aboard and stowed, but during the evolution of 'fishing', one of the sailors fell from the cathead into the sea. With sail set and the vessel already moving, as the sea boat was being lowered over the side the slings slipped, and suddenly there were an additional twelve men floundering in the water, of whom a midshipman and two seamen drowned, being unable to swim. A second boat was lowered, which rescued the remainder, including the man responsible for the entire misadventure, but by now the *Venerable* had lost the

Victim of a North Sea gale, the Polish trawler *Nurzec* lies stranded on the Murcar Sands, off Aberdeen, Scotland on 5 January 1974. Her captain, Tym Bartczak is here shown being rescued by breeches-buoy; four other members of his crew lost their lives *(Eric Collins collection)*

The oldest vessel in the British merchant service at the time of her loss, the tanker *Hemsley I* lies a total wreck in Fox's Cove, west of Treyarnon Bay, North Cornwall, on 12 May 1969. Built for the Admiralty in 1916, after going ashore in Cornwall, in dense fog, her position was reported by her captain as being 'near the Lizard', whereas in fact she was some sixty miles north and on the other coast! *(RLC)*

With a thirty-foot-long gash in her starboard side and other extensive hull damage, the 11,000-ton tanker *Dona Marika* lies stranded beneath cliffs near Milford Haven, Dyfed, South Wales, after going ashore on 6 August 1973 *(Basil James)*

wind. Taken aback, she drifted to leeward and down on to Paignton Ledges, on Roundham Head, where she stranded. Only the *Goliath* and *Impeteaux*, 4th- and 3rd-rate men o' war respectively, heard the *Venerable*'s distress guns. Turning back, they lowered all their boats, thinking the warship could be towed clear. Unfortunately, a freshening onshore wind had already driven the 1,669-ton ship well ashore, where she was already beating out her bottom planks. Her captain ordered the masts cut down, and had they fallen shoreward as intended, to form a series of 'bridges' with the land, escape for the crew would have been easy; as things were, they fell seaward.

The wind steadily increased to gale force, the waves pounding the wreck which was now on its beam ends. Some of the more agile crew members clambered along the bowsprit, dropping off on to rocks, whence they reached land. Others reached safety in the ship's boats. The majority owed their lives to the cutter *Frisk*, which anchored close to the wreck, taking off all but the last seventeen men, who declared they would rather die than desert their captain or ship. As the forecastle went underwater in the rising tide, so Captain Hunter finally conceded that he should leave, and by 6 am next morning, the *Venerable* was deserted, after which she broke in two. In *An Historical Survey of Torquay*, the author suggests that a drunken marine was left to his fate aboard the man o' war, having been caught red-handed plundering the officers' cabins and stealing wine after the ship stranded. Whilst the incident is true, the marine was in fact removed ashore, appearing at a court-martial held on board *El Salvador del Mundo* in Plymouth; he was found guilty and sentenced to receive 200 lashes by 'flogging round the fleet'. Whether or not he survived his harsh punishment is not recorded in contemporary newspapers. Of the 555 men aboard the *Venerable*, the total saved accounted for 547, which with three known to have been drowned before the wreck, suggests that perhaps five took advantage of the situation, and deserted. Not a single boat put out from Torquay, Paignton or Brixham to help save the crew, the majority of locals being far too busy misappropriating what ever they could lay their hands on, of the wreckage and effects washed ashore. Sixteen hours after the last man had left the wreck, nothing showed above the surface, which, considering the huge bulk of such a vessel, and the mass of timber in her construction, is quite remarkable. Despite a guard on the foreshore, consisting of Sea Fensibles, Coast Watchers, Volunteers, Marines from the *Impeteaux* and local cavalry, 'wicked fellows are base enough to venture out in the nite to plunder', and a great deal was stolen. The following spring, the sloop *Daniel* arrived on site from the Isles of Scilly, under orders from the Board of Ordnance to salvage the cannon and fittings from the wreck of the *Venerable*, having already been engaged in similar work on the *Colossus*.

Despite changes in the fortunes of the many East India companies already mentioned, the Dutch and English organisations were still transporting large sums of specie well into the 1800s. One such ship was the *Earl of Abergavenny*, outward bound from London to Bengal and China, whose intended voyage ended outside Weymouth harbour, in 60ft of water. In convoy with four other Company vessels, escorted by the frigate *Weymouth*, they called at Portsmouth, then proceeded down channel. Of 1,200 tons, the *Abergavenny* was a particularly large ship, with a reputation gained over three previous passages to the Far East, of extreme passenger comfort. Her captain, John Wordsworth, brother of the poet, followed in the steps of his uncle, who also had commanded the same vessel. Far from being a superstitious man, several times he remarked on feelings of apprehension before sailing, feelings so strong he deliberately delayed and even attempted to avoid the customary farewell visit to the Directors at East India House, where final instructions and dispatches were handed over. As the *Abergavenny* left Portsmouth on 3 February 1805, she carried on board as varied a collection of humans as can be imagined. There were 402 persons in all, comprising 160 seamen, 100 King's Troops, 59 East India

Company soldiers, 32 Chinese, and 60 passengers of both sexes, including children. Passing the Isle of Wight to the west, through the Needles Channel, the small fleet became separated from its escort, and consequently 'lay-to' all next day, but still the *Weymouth* failed to appear. Consequently, it was agreed that Captain Clarke of the *Wexford* should assume the role of Commodore, and lead them into Portland Roads to await the warship.

At approximately 3.30 pm on 5 February, a pilot boarded the *Abergavenny*, and with a strong wind on her port quarter, she stood in for the anchorage. When close to the Shambles Bank, a large area of shallow rock and sand, the wind dropped and the tide swept her ashore, where she remained for an hour. At first it appeared that there was no damage to the hull, but on the flood tide, when she floated clear, the ship's carpenter discovered a leak, and soon the water level in the hold had risen from 6in to 6ft. A boat was lowered and manned by the purser, third mate and six seamen, who set off for the shore to fetch help, but were never seen again. It was 9 pm before the captain advised the passengers that the *Abergavenny* was in danger of foundering, by which time the crew were in a state of mutiny, demanding the key to the spirit locker. Only the presence of an officer armed with a brace of pistols kept them from making a forceful entry. As the Indiaman wallowed north towards the beach at Weymouth, a pilot sloop appeared on the scene, rescuing three male and two female passengers, but for reasons unknown neither returned to the wreck, nor apparently alerted the authorities ashore as to the situation. It really was a most incredible situation; one of the nation's most valuable East Indiamen, leased to the largest trading organisation in the world, was sinking within earshot of a large seaport, and hardly a soul aware of the situation, despite distress signals being fired. At eleven o'clock that evening, the *Abergavenny* gave a lurch and went down, settling upright on the seabed in twelve fathoms, her mainmast top clear of the waves. Those who managed to save themselves either scrambled into the longboat, which floated from off the mainhatch, or else clambered up the shrouds, clear of the breakers. In due course, a number of Weymouth boats appeared, but were more interested in salvage, and in fact saved not one life between them. Providentially, a large sloop came alongside, attracted by cries for help. In three trips to Weymouth, she saved some sixty sailors and troops, there being no passengers left alive. As 4th Officer Gilpin, the last crew member to leave the wreck, stepped aboard the sloop which started for the shore, he pointed back and exclaimed that there was still someone in the rigging. Frozen stiff and almost helpless, a sergeant of the 22nd Regiment was found in the topmast rigging, and had to be carried into the boat, but died from exposure within four hours. A second rescue was attempted when Mr Baggot, the ship's 1st Officer, was sighted in the water, clinging to wreckage. He refused all help until a female passenger, also in the water, was taken aboard first. Leaving the security of his float, he swam towards her, but in attempting to drag her to safety, both went under and drowned.

Soon after the *Abergavenny* foundered, her spar deck burst upward with the pressure of trapped air in the hold, which released all the passengers' baggage, as well as items of cargo and ship's stores, which littered the beaches for miles. When the final reckoning was made, the mass burial of eighty bodies in one grave being the largest, it was found that 247 lives had been lost, and hence only 155 had escaped, of whom only five were passengers. Since the ship carried £70,000 in dollars as trading revenue, every effort was made by the company to save the money and cargo. To this end, the services of two early 'wrack-men' were employed, 'the ingenious Mr Tomkins and his diving bell', and later the famous salvor Braithwaithe, who between them recovered almost every coin. The remains of the *Earl of Abergavenny* can still be found on a sandy bottom, not far from Weymouth harbour, and received the attention of at least one group of divers during the summer of 1980, who intended to make the wreck an underwater archaeological project.

The five-year period to 1810 following the loss of the

Abergavenny saw a proliferation of shipwrecks, but generally with only occasional glimpses of the facts recorded for posterity in provincial newspapers or personal correspondence. On 6 November 1806, news was received from Weymouth of a large brig, London to Liverpool, wrecked on Portland beach, and one month later the American ship *Betsey*, New York to Amsterdam with sugar, coffee and indigo, went to pieces in Plymouth Sound. Captured as a prize vessel by the privateer *Lion*, she drove ashore between 'Cobler's Reach and Withy Hedge', fell on her side and became a total wreck. Her captain and six men got ashore by swimming through the surf, but a boat full of others overturned and all drowned. Local trawl boats were immediately hired to salvage her cargo, valued at £20,000. Meanwhile, on the east coast, the *Norfolk Mercury* in February 1807 reported: 'The storm in the night between Tuesday and Wednesday has been attended with effects the most fatal upon our coast, those unfortunate ships caught under sail had their canvas blown to atoms, or were dismasted. A horrid scene presented itself at daybreak, two vessels laying totally wrecked on the Scroby (Sands), their crews perished; another, after having been fast near four hours got off and went to southward. One vessel foundered at anchor, and the crew trusted to the frail chance of saving their lives in their boat, and left the vessel a few minutes before she went down. After passing through a small raging sea, in attempting to reach the harbour (Gt Yarmouth), the boat was oversett, and they were numbered with the dead.' Elsewhere on the same coast, vessels were stranded at Bacton, Trimingham, and at Happisburgh, a Revenue cutter being lost at the latter with all hands, and between there and Cromer, nine craft were ashore on 12 miles of coast. A merchantman running for the shelter of Yarmouth harbour, collided with HM brig *Snipe*, of 12 guns, lying at anchor in the Roads. Both vessels foundered, with an appalling loss of life, the former with ninety-three drowned, including French prisoners-of-war, women and children. *Snipe* went ashore at Gorleston, a little to the south of the entrance, from where attempts were made to float a line out to the wreck, which only resulted in the death of Phineas Grimble, a local pilot, who became entangled in the rope on the shore. Of the ninety-two people aboard the man o' war, only twenty survived the ordeal.

This particular incident is accredited with having inspired Captain George Manby, an artilleryman barrack master at the Yarmouth Depot, to conceive the idea of a line-carrying mortar, which subsequently saved many thousands of lives. Although innovative when used in connection with ship-wrecks, the basic idea was not entirely original, since a Lieutenant John Bell, a sergeant in 1791 at the time of his experiments at Woolwich, had already proven the viability of such an idea. Although it may have been a mere chance, the fact that both men were in the Royal Artillery cannot be overlooked, and that Manby may well have witnessed or heard of Bell's experiments but not realised their potential until sixteen years later, when he stood on the cliffs overlook-ing the wreck of the *Snipe*. It is also quite remarkable that during that same year, 1807, two men, working independently and in widely separated locations, were both sufficiently moved by shipwreck incidents to devote all their energy to differing apparatus to fire a line from the land across a wreck, or vice versa. Although the Manby Mortar Apparatus, as it became known, was the first in general use around the British Isles, the rocket apparatus invented by Henry Trengrouse of Helston, Cornwall, eventually proved superior. A modern-day version, little-changed in principle since its origin, is currently standard issue to HM Coastguard Cliff Rescue Teams.

Although it is generally accepted that it was the wreck of the frigate *Anson* that fired the enthusiasm of Trengrouse, it was more probably the combination of two equally tragic wrecks in close proximity that did so. The first of these was the government-hired transport *James & Rebecca*, returning home with a squadron of the 9th Light Dragoons, from General Whitelock's disastrous Buenos Aires expedition.

Shortly before midnight on 6 November 1807, she struck below Halsferran cliff, south-east of the village of Gunwalloe, in Mount's Bay, Cornwall. Of the 200 people aboard, over half were saved by a rope chair running on a taut hawser between mizzen mast and clifftop. She broke up at 11 am next day, and ten sailors, twenty-eight troopers and three children drowned. This incident took place less than 5 miles from Helston, and is certainly one of the shipping losses to which Trengrouse refers when he wrote of 'such tragic sea losses and waste of human life'. Seven weeks later, just before dawn on 29 December, the 44-gun, 5th-rate *Anson*, Captain Lydiard, seeking shelter from a gale while on Channel blockade duty, parted from her last remaining anchor and went ashore on Loe Bar, about a mile from Porthleven. With her head to the south east, she broached-to on the rapidly shelving shingle beach. Its treacherous underlying reefs of rock have torn the bottom out of every wooden vessel, and a few steel ones as well, which have been unfortunate enough to assume that Loe Bar represented a safe place to beach a vessel. Her mainmast fell shoreward forming a bridge over which many escaped, but still 120 lives were lost. Henry Trengrouse stood on the cliff-top overlooking the scene, horrified at the seemingly helpless situation of the poor wretches on board, when dry land and salvation were only yards away, and the only means whereby a line could be passed was for someone to risk their life swimming between the ship and shore.

Although trials of the Manby Apparatus, which consisted of a miniature, light-weight mortar gun which fired modified spherical iron shot, to which was connected a light line, were completed to the satisfaction of the Board of Ordnance by the end of 1807, it still required an actual wreck incident to prove its worth. Such an opportunity presented itself on 12 February 1808. The brig *Elizabeth* of Plymouth was seen in distress, 150yds off Yarmouth beach in Norfolk, in a north-easterly gale. All attempts to launch boats through the surf proved fruitless, and eventually only the new apparatus stood between the crew's rescue and a watery grave. On the first firing, the shot fell clean across the wreck, and soon the seamen were hauling a boat out from the shore which enabled them to reach safety. By the end of 1810, over seventy lives had been saved by the apparatus in Norfolk alone. By the time the Norfolk Association for Saving the Lives of Shipwrecked Mariners was formed in 1823, more than 250 people owed their lives to Manby's invention. Twenty years after the *Snipe* incident this had reached 324, discounting those rescued in other counties.

It took Trengrouse a great many years to perfect his invention, which was a rocket-propelled line-throwing apparatus, lighter and cheaper than Manby's, which could be used equally well from ship or shore. Since the necessary investment was entirely his own private money, without access to government stores and gunpowder enjoyed by Captain Manby, it was 1818 before his device was finally accepted into general service, being considered the superior of the two after comparison trials. The letter which approved of the Trengrouse apparatus, written by Rear Admiral Sir Charles Rowley from on board *Bulwark* in the Medway on 5 March 1818 read:

Sir, you will be pleased to acquaint my Lords Commissioners of the Admiralty, that in compliance with their Lordships' directions of the 24th ultimo, I attended at Woolwich on the 28th, with Captain Gore of His Majesty's sloop *Doterel*, and Captain Ross of Deptford; and met the Committee of Colonels and Field Officers of Artillery, convened for the purpose of inspecting an Apparatus invented by Mr Trengrouse, for preserving lives and property in cases of Shipwreck, by means of a Rocket; —when Mr Trengrouse exhibited his Apparatus, consisting of a section of a tube or cylinder, which is fitted to the barrel of a musket by a bayonet socket; a rocket, with a line attached to its stick, is so placed in it, that its priming receives fire immediately from the barrel.

The following experiments were made:—

First. A small rocket of 8oz fixed as described, was fired to the distance of one hundred and eighty yards.

One of six German submarines sunk off Falmouth, near Pendennis Point in 1921 *(RLC)*

The wreck of the trawler *Jeanne* between Runswick and Whitby, Yorkshire, on 16 February 1932, in which three were drowned. The ship's lifeboat lies smashed to pieces on the foreshore *(RLC)*

Victim of the Seven Stones Reef, the Rumanian fish factory ship *Rarau*, which stranded on 29 September 1976. This same set of rocks, midway between Land's End and the Isles of Scilly, caused the wreck of the tanker *Torrey Canyon* in addition to countless others *(F.E. Gibson)*

The 487 tons gross MV *Greenhaven* lies upside down and wrecked on Roarurish reef, near Burtonport, Co Donegal, Ireland, 1 March 1956 *(MOD – Navy)*

The 500-ton motor coaster *Hindlea*, which dragged ashore near Moelfre, on the north coast of Anglesey, on 27 October 1959. By coincidence, it was a gale with winds in excess of 100mph which put her ashore, in almost exactly the same place as the *Royal Charter* was lost in similar conditions, 100 years and one day earlier *(RLC)*

Second. A pound rocket was fired in the same manner, which ranged four hundred and fifty yards; the line broke at one hundred and fifty yards, owing to a knot in it.

Third. A pound rocket was fired from a wooden frame, at an elevation of 50° and ranged two hundred and twelve yards. The line used with the above three pounds, was a mackerel line.

Fourth. A 4oz rocket was fired from the musket to a distance of one hundred and twelve yards, with a line called a mackerel snood.

The Committee were of opinion, That Mr Trengrouse's mode appears to them to be the best that has been suggested for the purpose of saving lives from Shipwreck, by gaining a communication with the shore; and, as far as the experiments went, it most perfectly answered what was proposed. I beg leave to suggest to my Lords Commissioners of the Admiralty, one of Mr Trengrouse's Apparatus being lodged in each of the Dock Yards, that the officers of the Navy may be made acquainted with the advantages of using a Rocket, as proposed by him, in time of necessity.

I have the honour to be, etc

C. Rowley

Rear Admiral

John Wilson Croker Esq
Secretary
Admiralty

Following a letter from the Admiralty secretary direct, requesting at what price Trengrouse would supply his Apparatus for the purpose of being issued to HM ships, their Lordships attempted to fob him off with a token payment, suggesting their own price as to the profit he might have made, which of course made no account of his expenses in development.

Admiralty Office
16th April 1818
Sir,

I am commanded by my Lords Commissioners of the Admiralty to acquaint you, that it had been their intention to purchase Twenty Sets of your apparatus for preserving lives and property in case of Shipwreck, by way of encouragement, but that the Committee of Naval and Artillery Officers, who lately witnessed experiments of it, having recommended that the Apparatus should be supplied to His Majesties ships from the Ordnance Department, rather than by you, and their Lordships being unwilling that you should suffer by this change of determination, they have directed the Navy Board, in lieu of purchasing the said number, to pay you the sum of Fifty Pounds, which their Lordships consider is a very liberal calculation of the profit you might have made in furnishing the Apparatus.

I am &c.

J. W. Croker

Mr H. Trengrouse
2 Villiers-Street, Strand.

Three ship losses of 25 January 1809 were to have strange repercussions during 1978. On the morning of 26 January, the inhabitants of Deal and Ramsgate were presented with the sight of three large vessels on the Goodwin Sands, each with only their foremasts standing, and waves breaking over their hulls. Two of them were English East Indiamen, namely the *Britannia* and *Admiral Gardner*, outward bound in company with the *Carnatic*, which had already rescued some crew members who had escaped in a boat. The third vessel was the brig *Apollo*, bound for Curacao, from which there was only one survivor, who had lashed himself to the rigging and declined the offer to save himself in the longboat. By the 31st of the month, all three had gone to pieces and the remains been engulfed in the sands. It was during the construction of the new hovercraft base at Dover that several dozen East India Company copper tokens, each bearing the denomination of 'X Cash', were first found in 1977. Discovered by children playing on the site, it became obvious that the trade tokens, all dated 1808, had been brought ashore with sand dredged from off the western edge of the South Goodwin. Several hundred were eventually recovered, a sad reminder of a tragedy acted out 168 years before.

It was December 1809 that a particularly unfortunate series of losses occurred in Seaford Bay, near Newhaven, Sussex. A convoy of twenty-three ships, escorted by the armed sloop *Harlequin*, were on passage up Channel from

Plymouth when they were overtaken by a severe south-westerly gale and dense fog. The sloop stood in for the land, her captain thinking that they would find some shelter behind Beachy Head, but in ignorance of their true position the *Harlequin* and six foremost vessels all ran ashore. Those stranded proved to be the *Weymouth*, 180 tons, with eleven crew and a cargo of cork, barilla and tobacco; the *Traveller*, eight crew, carrying shumac and fruit; *Albion*, nine crew and a general cargo; *Unice*, ten crew, carrying cotton; *February*, 460 tons, sixteen crew, in ballast; *Midbedach*, 359 tons, fourteen crew, with a general cargo, and the escort vessel, commanded by Lieutenant Anstruther RN. Daybreak showed three other ships in the convoy ashore further up the coast, and every one of the ten stranded that night became a total wreck, with a very heavy loss of life.

The history of the first steamship to operate commercially in Europe, the *Comet*, has a place in this chapter since both it and its successor, *Comet II*, were wrecked in Scotland. Built at Port Glasgow in 1811/12 to the order of John Bell, the 40.25ft, 30-ton craft acquired its name after the great comet of 1811. In August 1812 she began her commercial operation on the Clyde, plying between Glasgow and Greenock, carrying passengers for a return first-class fare of four shillings, or second-class for three shillings. Financially unsuccessful, due to the general reluctance of the public to trust this new mode of transport, Bell put the little steamer to 'jaunting', which in modern terms would be better described as 'excursion trips'. These took the *Comet* all over the coasts of Great Britain. Twelve months later, with steam at sea now well accepted, no fewer than nine new steamships were launched on the Clyde; by the end of 1815 a total of twenty-six had been built and were now operating on the Forth, Tay, Mersey, Thames, Avon, Yare, Trent, Tyne and in Eire. The *Comet* met its end whilst on an excursion, stranded on the point of Craignish Rock, Dorishmore, at 4.30 pm on 18 December 1820, whilst plying between Fort William and Glasgow. The forward part of the vessel containing the 8–10hp engine remained fast on the rocks, but the after end, which broke free, drifted away into the Corrievreckan whirlpool and was never seen again. Her steam engine was salvaged, and for several years afterwards drove machinery in MacLellan's coachbuilding works in Miller Street, Glasgow. It then served for a while in a Greenock brewery, finally being purchased by Robert Napier in 1862, who presented it to the Kensington Science Museum, London, where it is still on display. Its namesake, *Comet II*, was run down and sunk in the Clyde on 21 October 1825. Commanded by Captain MacInnes, *Comet II* left Inverness at 6 am on the 18th, and steaming via the Caledonian Canal reached Fort William, where the passengers disembarked and slept ashore. On the following day, the Crinan Canal was navigated in the same manner, and emerging from the Kyles of Bute, the steamer proceeded up the Clyde. At 2 am on the 21st, she was abeam of Kempoch Point, a headland between the Cloch lighthouse and Gourock, but without a single navigation light displayed, and a jib sail preventing all but the lookout from a forward view. As soon as the steamer *Ayr* was sighted coming straight for them, the *Comet*'s lookout shouted to his pilot to put the wheel to starboard. This command was heard so clearly by the helmsman of the other vessel that he assumed it applied to him, and, putting his wheel over, allowed both craft to turn towards each other. In consequence, the steamers collided, the starboard bow of the *Comet* was stove in, and she sank in two minutes. Exactly how many were on board was not known with any certainty (the purser drowned). In any case, no proper account was kept of the many individuals that joined or left the ferry *en route*, but the total was presumed to be sixty or seventy. All the passengers except nine drowned, and, of the crew, only her master and pilot survived. Following the collision, the paddles of the *Ayr* were put in reverse, she backed off, turned and set off for Greenock, leaving the *Comet* and those aboard to their fate. The hull of the *Comet* was eventually raised and beached, which revived memories of the loss of the *Catherine*, of Iona, which had been run down and sunk by the steamboat *Hercules* in similar circumstances on 10 August 1822. In this accident, four survived out of forty-six persons.

The coast of North Wales, although receiving little mention to date, had a horrifying record of losses, particularly in the 1830/40 period. On one day alone in 1844, ten vessels were driven ashore near Porth-Dinllaen, whilst official figures for 1844/58 state that eighty-seven ships were total losses in the Caernarvon Bay area alone. An early steam packet wrecked on Dutchman's Bank on 17 August 1831 is typical of the many disasters in the vicinity of the Great Orme Head. The *Rothesay Castle* was offering the public short sea excursions between Liverpool and Beaumaris, on Anglesey, and after some frantic touting by the captain, she sailed with 150 passengers aboard. Built in 1816, she was grossly underpowered, worn out, leaky, ill-equipped, and altogether totally unsuitable and unseaworthy for such passenger service. Several men had refused to sail in her as crew, and one man in particular even used this as proof of his sanity before the Manchester Commissioners in Lucnay, which was accepted! Despite a small brass band on deck, attempting to enliven everyone's spirits by playing a well-known air of the period— 'Cheer Up, Cheer Up'—the passengers were soon to regret their decision to join the *Rothesay Castle*.

Slowly she clanked and rattled her way out to sea, and with the sea now rough and most of the passengers pleading to be returned to Liverpool, the captain was found at the saloon table drunk. Despite widespread seasickness, water ankle deep in the stokehold, and partially choked pumps, he refused to turn back. The male passengers offered to bale her out with buckets, but were told there had only been one on board, and that had been lost overboard. After steaming for ten hours, during which time they covered only 36 miles, the steamer struck the unseen Dutchmans Bank, close to Great Orme Head. It was impossible to go astern, since the rising water had extinguished the boiler fire, so the vessel bumped its way along the back edge for a full mile, before breaking in two. First the funnel collapsed, bringing down the mast, which in turn struck and killed the drunken captain; then the paddle boxes broke away. Several passengers threw themselves into the sea to swim ashore, since Puffin Island was reasonably close at hand, but all perished. A further forty passengers went over the side with the weather paddle box, and fifty more when the entire quarterdeck broke free and drifted away. Only twenty survived the wreck, the majority of the dead being interred in Beaumaris churchyard. When told that the *Rothesay Castle* had been wrecked, one of the local boatmen who launched to rescue some survivors exclaimed, 'Ah! I knew that would be the end of her. I left her last week for that very reason!'

It was incidents such as the loss of the *Rothesay Castle*, which quite patently was unfit to have been in service, that caused the British Government to call for a full-scale and searching investigation into the many aspects of shipwreck. Consequently, on 1 July 1836, the Select Committee on Shipwreck was formed, and one of the first witnesses called concerning lighthouses was William Bush, who had been attempting to put a permanent beacon on the Goodwin Sands. By 1838, they had collected a mass of statistics regarding wooden ships lost, then steamers, then wood versus iron, the qualification of pilots, harbours of refuge, and many other aspects. Their final report, with its hundreds of recommendations, which were to be far-reaching in their consequences, could not avert still more terrible shipwrecks such as the *Floridan*, in which 174 German emigrants died. On 28 February 1849, a south-westerly gale accompanied by snow was affecting the entire south coast of the country, and the 500-ton barque, bound for America, was close inshore and lost. With nothing to be seen in any direction but swirling snow, she plunged headlong into the Long Sand at the mouth of the Thames Estuary, and immediately filled with water. Her passengers, mostly young and respectable agricultural mechanics and labourers, unwittingly contributed to their fate, by gross hindrance of the crew. Attempts to launch boats resulted in them being cut loose, or else being dropped in their panic. Boats which were launched were immediately swamped by the rush of people, who fought each other for a place. When the *Floridan* at last broke in two, all her cargo burst out, the boxes and bales smashing limbs and knocking people overboard. For two days and nights, a diminishing number of survivors clung to the wreckage, praying for salvation, as one by one they succumbed to exhaustion and cold. Help finally appeared in the form of the *Petrel*, a small cutter, which darted close in and took off three sailors and one male passenger, the only survivors. The young German was landed at Harwich and taken to hospital, but he had lost his reason, and was condemned to a mental institution for life as a result of that wreck.

6

WILD WIND AND BREAKERS, THEIR FUNERAL DIRGE

1850–1899

A recurrent feature of nineteenth-century shipwrecks was the often disproportionate number of people drowned to those saved, at almost every incident. With the introduction of iron vessels and steam propulsion, the numbers of passengers carried aboard even relatively small craft increased often out of all reasonable proportion, and in the case of most emigrant ships was criminal. In the late twentieth century, an inability to swim is the exception rather than the rule, hence it is difficult to imagine an era when less than ten percent of the population could keep themselves afloat in the sea. Such was the situation in the nineteenth century, aggravated by a total lack of legislation concerning the provision of lifeboats, life-jackets and other buoyancy aids on board ships in the event of accident. A passenger vessel carrying 500 people would probably have a lifeboat capacity sufficient only to save 100 people, and that assuming none of them were damaged, and all could be safely launched. Consequently, the loss of life among passengers and crew alike in a shipwreck was un-naturally high. Perhaps no period in the maritime history of the British Isles illustrated this fact more clearly than that between 1850 and 1899, which began with a spate of particu-larly tragic losses on the coast of Scotland and Ireland.

The 333-ton steam packet *Queen Victoria*, which plied regularly as a ferry between Dublin and Liverpool, carried twenty-five crew and 100 passengers when she sailed for

Ireland on 14 February 1853. A majority of the men were cattle dealers returning from the Liverpool markets. At 2 am on the 15th, those of the crew on watch were searching the horizon ahead for the approach lights to Dublin Bay, when a blinding snowstorm reduced visibility to a few yards, but not before a faint light was sighted which was assumed to be the Baily lighthouse. The obvious and seamanlike course of action in such circumstances was to reduce speed or stoꞋ until the squall passed, but the only concession made by the mate was to join the lookout on the forecastle. He arrived at the bow in time to see the high cliffs of Howth island loom up ahead, then the packet plunged headlong into the rocks at full speed, throwing those below decks from their bunks. Hurrying from his cabin, the captain ordered the engine to full-astern, and backed the vessel off into deep water, but with the sea pouring in through torn plates, he hastily changed his mind, and deliberately drove her ashore again to avoid foundering. Panic and confusion swept through the passengers who refused to obey the captain's orders to 'be quiet', and 'Remain calm'. They crowded on deck, some naked, some in night attire, fighting to get up the companionways from below, then screaming and praying to be allowed back again when they realised their children or belongings had been left behind. An eyewitness described the scene as 'appalling, enough to unnerve the stoutest heart. The distress of the poor creatures was dreadful, I never saw anything to equal the horrors of that scene and I trust in God I may never be doomed to witness another like it'.

Someone shouted, 'For God's sake get out the boats!', and a great mass surged towards the starboard quarter boat and attempted to board. The combined weight of too many occupants caused it to break from its davits, whereupon it fell into the sea and everyone aboard drowned. The port boat got away safely, but with only seventeen aboard, and would never have reached the nearby steamship *Roscommon* had not a young boy stuck his finger in the unstoppered plug-hole and kept it there. On returning to the wreck, the port boat found only her masts above water. A further seventeen were rescued from the rigging, while eight others swam ashore, the total number drowned being eighty-three. Although it had no bearing on the mate's negligence in failing to reduce speed, or use the lead and line when close to land, the Board of Trade inquiry considered that the dimness of the Baily light was a contributory factor. Their investigations proved that the keeper had in fact gone to bed after lighting the lantern, instead of maintaining his watch, allowing the lamp to burn low and snow to obscure the glass completely.

With almost 400 lives lost, the worst emigrant ship accident of 1853 concerned the *Annie Jane*, of Liverpool, lost on Isle Vatersa amongst the Hebrides on 29 September. Bound for Montreal with 450 passengers, mostly Irish families seeking a new life in Canada, the sailing ship left her home port on the 9th, returned with severe storm damage hours later, sailed a second time after repairs only to be completely dismasted thirty-six hours later in a force eleven storm. Fortunately, of the 100 or so passengers from Glasgow and West Scotland, a proportion were skilled carpenters and artisans, all with tool chests aboard, and in no time the spare mainyard was turned into a jury rigged mast. Driven as far north as 60° latitude by continuous gales, the first land sighted was Barra Head, the southernmost island of the Hebrides group. Measuring only 6 miles long and 2½ wide, there was hardly a place in Scotland from which survivors of a shipwreck were less likely to be rescued. Sight of Barra Head, which holds the highest lighthouse in the British Isles, the top reaching to 680ft, gave all forty-five crew members on deck hope that they could anchor in its lee, but the ship was driven into a sandy bay where she stranded. Apart from a few men who remained on deck, the majority of the passengers were below asleep, and their reaction to the fearful hammer-like blows of rocks against the hull was a re-enactment of the panic witnessed aboard the *Queen Victoria*. Women dashed about screaming, others clung to their menfolk or belongings, with everyone making a great deal of noise.

As the wreck slewed beam on to the sea, one huge wave broke over her deck, carrying an estimated 100 people to a watery grave, and with them went all the boats, the ship's bulwarks and loose gear. Further waves caused the wreck to break into three sections, which allowed the sea to get amongst her cargo of railway lines, and as a result a huddle of passengers between the stumps of the main and mizzen masts were crushed and mutilated. Those who survived (and there were precious few, since the final count showed that 393 had lost their lives) found their way to the only farm, where food and shelter were provided. Next day, the most pressing problem concerned the burial of the dead, and with no suitable timber available from which to make coffins, the dead were carried slung over men's shoulders for the ten long miles to the only burial ground. Here they were laid to rest in huge pits, a total of 260 being dealt with in the first three days.

It was another Mersey-built emigrant ship, the 1,979-ton, iron full-rigged ship *Tayleur*, which claimed 290 lives on her maiden voyage, when she was wrecked on the Nose of Lambay Island, Co Dublin. With her figurehead a likeness of her builder, from whom she derived her name, the *Tayleur* left Liverpool on Thursday 19 January 1854, with 496 passengers and thirty-two crew, bound for Montreal. Heading south down the Irish Sea, all went well for two days. Then fog set in and soon the ship was close inshore and drifting towards the land. Alarmed at the proximity of danger, the passengers crowded on deck, hampering the crew in their duties and making so much noise that it was impossible for the officers to transmit orders. Fighting his way to the forecastle, the master ordered both anchors dropped, but still the wind and sea relentlessly pushed her towards the high cliffs of Lambay Island. Finally, both cables parted, the ship drove beam on to the rocks at the base of the cliffs, and began to beat on the bottom. Her position was in fact so close to shore, that a number of passengers actually jumped ashore, then a plank was positioned between the bulwark and some rocks, and some literally walked to safety. Most of the Lascars and Chinese amongst the crew clambered ashore and dashed off, with no attempt to assist those left behind. Then part of the wreck collapsed, she lurched away from the land, and the only means of getting off was by swinging hand over hand across a number of ropes secured between the rigging and rock outcrops. Several young Irish women managed to get half way, then lost their strength and fell into the sea, and at the subsequent inquiry it was noticeable that of the 200 females aboard, only three survived. Again, an eyewitness report of events was quoted in a provincial newspaper as saying,

> The scene was truly awful. The most desperate struggles for life were made by the wretched passengers great numbers of whom jumped overboard in the vain hope of reaching land, and the ropes crowded by hundreds who, in their eagerness, terror and confusion, frustrated each other's efforts for self-preservation. Many of the females would get part way, and then become unable to proceed further, and after clinging to the rope, would be forced from their hold by the press of those who came after.

The ship's stern then went underwater as the wreck began to collapse, and the ropes to the shore parted. Every wave now claimed one or more victims, even whole groups of people going overboard. Eventually the coastguards arrived, and after saving two men ruddled in the rigging, led the survivors to the castle of Lord Talbot, whose steward served oatmeal and potatoes, and later killed a pig for roasting. Later, the Board of Trade appointed jury set down that the owners of the *Tayleur* were guilty of highly culpable neglect in permitting the ship to sail without properly swung compasses, and for not carrying out sea trials to ascertain the degree of helm control available. But this was a period when 'coffin' ships existed in their hundreds, when there was a lot of money to be made from the government and poor, in transporting people to the colonies, and ship owners knew only too well, that as with everything, nothing lasts for ever.

Although such Board of Trade inquiries into the loss of lives and vessels were properly conducted affairs, usually held before Justices of the Peace or Magistrates, who had the power to deprive a man of his seagoing certificates of competency, and hence his livelihood, at times their verdict appeared hard and unjust. A typical example was the incident leading to the loss of the 453-ton sailing vessel *Saxon King*, of London, on 9 January 1859, which would appear to have warranted some leniency. She left Samarang for Cork, for orders, calling there on the 6th, leaving for Glasgow two days later. The South Rock Reef, two miles off the coast of Co Down, in the Irish Channel, was sighted bearing due north. With a course set to clear the rocks by a narrow margin, five minutes later the vessel struck some sort of submerged reef. Assistance was obtained from some local fishermen, and after a portion of the cargo had been thrown over the side, she was refloated, and an attempt made to reach Glasgow. In a near waterlogged condition, it was impossible to steer her, and having lost all her principal sail in a gale, she was anchored off Corsewall Point, 9 miles north of Stranraer. Her crew decided that they had had enough. Despite their knowledge that she was sinking, they abandoned the vessel with Captain Deans and two fishermen aboard, leaving them to their fate. A short while later the *Saxon King* did in fact founder and became a total loss, but the three men aboard were rescued. Only at the inquiry was it made public that there had been a bitter dispute between the master and mate, the latter refusing to perform any further duties. This left Captain Deans as the only officer capable of keeping the deck watch, as well as being responsible for all the navigation. At the time of her sinking, he had been on watch for more than twenty-six hours without a break or rest, and was exhausted. His superiors decided that he had committed a serious error of judgment in miscalculating the distance between his ship and the South Reef Rock lightvessel, and for not using the lead and line. The unfortunate master had his certificate suspended for three months, in circumstances where some degree of compassion would have been justified.

On the same day that the brigantine *Dusty Miller* was lost with all hands—28 April 1859, near Lambay, and close to the wreck of the *Queen Victoria* of 1853—the American owned *Pomone* was wrecked on Blackwater Bank. With the loss of 424 lives (since only twenty sailors, the 3rd Mate and three passengers survived out of a total of 448 aboard), it was the worst emigrant vessel disaster of the century in British waters, overshadowed only by the homeward bound *Royal Charter*, in which 446 lost their lives. The 1,500-ton ship *Pomone* left Liverpool with her human cargo in the same buoyant mood as that of thousands of emigrants before, and while some took to their bunks in discreet submission to seasickness, the majority were celebrating by dancing to a fiddler on deck, as they headed for the open sea and a new life—or so they thought. The *Pomone* went headlong to her destruction, since near the Tuskar Rock, off Carnsore Point, the most south-easterly part of Co Wexford and Eire, she ran onto a sandbank. Stopped dead in her forward movement, heavy seas whipped up by a gale broke over the deck, sweeping all before them and flooding the hold. Somehow the vessel held together, but at daybreak, as each boat was launched, so it was dashed to pieces and the occupants drowned. Only the one boat remaining on the port side managed to get away, with twenty-four occupants, who turned out to be the sole survivors eventually. As the tide rose and the wreck became more buoyant, the *Pomone* slipped off the bank, and sometime later sank, but not one individual survived to give an account of those last hours. That the bodies of the dead washed ashore were plundered was understandable, the Irish have never had it easy, and the 1850s were particularly hard times. Whether or not they really were 'too barbarous for credence', as one reporter wrote, is impossible to say. Because several corpses were found naked, it was assumed their clothes had been stolen, and because they were found floating close to the shore, that the bodies had been thrown back to conceal the evidence. When the storm abated, the Liverpool Salvage Association sent divers to examine the wreck. From the fore-part of the *Pomone*, between decks, almost 300 bodies were recovered, proving that in her last moments, few were able to gain the upper deck before she plunged to the bottom.

If these tragedies shocked the nation, then the wreck of the *Royal Charter* left it stunned, for this was one of the greatest peacetime disasters in British history. That she was lost at the very end of a journey which had taken her half way round the world and back was bad enough; that she should be wrecked only hours from her destination of Liverpool, and then within 50 feet of the shore, was almost incomprehensible. Of the 500 persons aboard, not a single woman or child survived, and only twenty men escaped, the majority of whom were badly injured. The 2,715-ton, 320ft-long steamer had been designed and built with the Australian emigrant trade in mind, and had been employed almost solely in this capacity, transporting people and stores out to the gold fields, discovered in 1851, and bringing back those who had either profited from their labours, or by contrast, had lost everything. Of a peculiar hybrid design, the *Royal Charter* was an iron-hulled, auxiliary sailing 'clipper', whose engine was used as little as possible; so that she had the mechanical advantages of a steamship coupled with the 'racehorse' characteristics of the fastest breed of sailing ships.

As she lay alongside at Melbourne on 26 August 1859, taking aboard passengers, cargo, luggage and stores, a small steamer moored alongside her port quarter, and a quantity of small wooden boxes were unloaded, and after the seals on each had been checked by Captain Taylor and an Australian Customs official, were stowed deep inside the hull in the strongroom. The boxes contained gold specie, valued at £322,440. But this probably represented less than half the true value of gold aboard, since dozens of private individuals carried personal fortunes. A Mrs Foster was one such individual, since she had £5,000 with her—not the proceeds of prospecting but profit from two hotels set up by her husband. This lady sailed on the *Royal Charter* outward bound, and completed her business in time to return aboard the same ship.

On 25 October 1859, the steamer was met off Bardsey Island by a tug, which passed over bundles of newspapers, also eleven riggers, seeking a return passage to Liverpool, having been 'steaming' crew on a vessel they had taken to Cardiff. Even when off Holyhead, a small island off Anglesey, apart from an unnatural look about the sky, there was no warning of the hurricane which was about to strike. It had already passed over Devon and Cornwall, but radio weather broadcasts were a thing of the future, so apart from the barometer there was no other indication. Even so, despite three such instruments on board the *Royal Charter*, the pressure drop when it came was so swift that there was little more than two hours' warning. By late afternoon all the signs of bad weather had manifested themselves, and it would still have been a simple matter for the steamer to have entered Holyhead harbour for shelter, but she was a 'crack' ship, and passage 'under sixty days' was the owner's proud boast.

At 10 pm, when off Point Lynas, the east-north-east gale increased to force ten, and within thirty minutes was at least force twelve or stronger, certainly with winds in excess of 100 mph. Caught in the grip of the ebbing tide, and the wind so strong the vessel was unable to make any headway, the only course of action was to anchor. But first one then the other cable parted, and the *Royal Charter* went adrift and headed for the rocks. When she struck, roller after roller tore into her, tearing the ship to pieces slowly, and waves over 60ft high claimed life after life. When it was all over, and the dead were buried, only then was the true intensity of the 1859 hurricane known, a holocaust which to this day is still called the '*Royal Charter* Gale'. During that one night alone, sixty-nine ships were wrecked around the British Isles, their size ranging from the *Royal Charter* down to the 16-ton smack *Richard & Elizabeth*, lost with all hands between Bude and Clovelly. In total, 795 people died in the sea that night, a number not exceeded by a single gale to date.

Of the many causes of shipwreck, drunkenness on the part of masters and captains is nothing new, as the old Board of Trade records clearly show. The Yarmouth sailing ship *Idalia* of 280 tons left Glasgow on 5 March 1861 for Le Havre,

A Danish motor coaster, the *Northwind*, forced ashore by a north-easterly gale on Hollacombe beach, between Paignton and Torquay, Devon, 22 December 1964. Her captain and five-man crew were rescued by breeches-buoy, and the vessel refloated several days later (*West of England Newspapers Ltd*)

The 2000-ton motor coaster *Shoreham*, ashore near Gull Rock, Mullion, on the south coast of Cornwall, 26 June 1979. Most of her cargo of limestone was pumped out or taken off by grab, and on 6 July she was refloated and towed to Falmouth (*RLC*)

South-west of the Bishop Rock, Isles of Scilly, the Panamanian motor vessel *Lutria* wallows in heavy seas as she slowly sinks. Her crew of twenty-eight were saved using their own boats, assisted by Sea King naval helicopters, 11 February 1974 *(Western Morning News)*

An unexpected visitor to Brighton was the motor vessel *Athina B*, a Greek owned vessel which stranded only yards from the busy promenade following a gale on 22 January 1980 *(London Express)*

Another victim of the treacherous west coast of Guernsey, the MV *Prosperity*, was wrecked and broke in two during a gale, on La Conchée reef, on 17 January 1974. She was a total loss, and all eighteen members of her crew drowned. The disaster took place while the *Elwood Mead* was still stranded, less than a mile away *(Richard Keen collection)*

with a cargo of iron, whisky, beer, and a crew of eleven men. It took her captain seven days to reach the Isle of Arran, a distance of forty-five miles, then he anchored in Lamlash Bay for a further week, leaving on the 19th. It later transpired that Captain John Plowman Ward was completely drunk the entire time. When approaching Holyhead the *Idalia* was seen to put about and head for the Irish coast, and with the senior officer totally incapable of any duty or reason and no-one else aboard capable of even basic navigation, they continued to sail the area at random. By the 21st the ship was back off Lamlash, and in endeavouring to enter harbour, the vessel went ashore. Other incidents followed, the drunken master cutting ropes, and throwing things at the crew as they escaped in a small boat. He was forceably disarmed of a loaded revolver by a coastguard officer. Captain Ward was later deprived of his seagoing certificate 'until such time as the Board of Trade were satisfied that he had learned sober habits'. A similar incident concerned the *Spy* of Jersey (John Edmund Hamon, Master). On passage from Demerara, the ship was off Beachy Head on 1 October 1862, making for the London docks, but ran ashore within 200 yards of the Dungeness lighthouse. Despite being so intoxicated that he was incapable of keeping his watch, the master had appeared on deck during the middle watch, and ordered a northerly course, which put her on the beach. All that day and the next, John Hamon was in a hopeless condition, refusing to hand over command, yet totally incapable of any rational thought, despite the fact his ship was going to pieces beneath his feet. As in the previous incident, 'amended habits' were expected by the authorities before he could again legally command a ship.

Possibly one of the strangest causes of shipwreck was the bizarre incident in which the crew of the *Lord Haddo* actually bored holes in the hull! She had left the Tyne for Cartegena on 24 January 1867, carrying a cargo of coal and coke. Her officers noticed that she was making some water, but no more than the pumps could handle easily. Three days out, after being pumped dry, the water level rose at an alarming level. With no stress of weather or reasonable cause for such a leak, the *Lord Haddo* was run ashore at Covehithe, near Southwold, in Suffolk, to prevent her foundering. Only then were the dozen or so auger holes found, which had been drilled from inside the hull, clean through her planking. It was later satisfactorily proven in court that the bosun had enticed the crew to scuttle the ship, and that after the sailors had been well plied with drink, they had bored holes in the port bow area. The only reasonable explanation was that the crew had received a month's wages in advance, and had 'wanted to make a short voyage of it'. The pilot and Chief Mate accused the master of cognisance, but the former's evidence was considered unreliable, since he had already perjured himself in a matter concerning his certificate.

Since silver or gold specie or 'treasure' is more often than not associated with historic or old wrecks, it may come as a surprise to know that silver coins can readily be found in the wreck of a steamship, off Southern Eire. The only vessel ever owned by the Liverpool and Mississippi Steamship Co was the iron, two-masted, flush-decked *Crescent City*, a craft of 2,105 tons gross, built at McMillan's yard, Dumbarton, in 1870. The *Crescent City* left New Orleans for the return passage of her maiden voyage on 12 January 1871, carrying 4,100 bales of cotton, a quantity of Indian corn, and forty boxes of coin, valued at $101,492. Once clear of the American coast, her engine was shut down and she sailed across the Atlantic until 8 February, when Captain Williams estimated that he was approximately 20 miles south of Kinsale. Under steam power again, they proceeded at full speed despite fog and bad visibility, and ran straight against the Dhulic Rock, off Galley Head lighthouse, Co Cork, and sank. Bad weather prevented the Liverpool Salvage Association from sending down divers until 25 February, when despite 'sweeping, grappling and diving in all directions', they were unable to locate the wreck. It took until the 30th to find her as she lay upright in 110ft, after which one cask and five boxes were salvaged, along with 170 loose dollars. The coins were in fact Mexican, not American, dollars, although their value at that time was similar. The total value of specie salvaged at the time is calculated to have been $59,847, which left some $41,553 or 41 percent of the total, presumably on the seabed. Today, with their low silver content, the coins are worth only a few pounds each, but even so, what was left could be worth some £124,659. Although inaccessible and subject to fierce tides, the site has received annual visits by divers over recent years, none of whom have left empty-handed. The sum remaining is now depleted, but at a conservative estimate at least £100,000-worth lie buried in the sand covering the rusting frames of the *Crescent City*, only a few hundred yards from the lighthouse.

Already cited as the cause of numerous shipwrecks and the downfall of ships' captains, alcohol was the cause of the death of twenty 'wreckers' on the Dorset coast on 25 November 1872. The iron sailing ship *Royal Adelaide* (Captain J. Hunter), was bound for Sydney from London, with thirty-two crew, thirty-five passengers, and a general cargo which included hundreds of casks and bottles of spirits. She drove ashore on Chesil beach in a heavy south-west gale, just close enough for a well-aimed rocket line, fired by the Wyke Rocket Brigade, to fall across her deck. By this means a rescue basket was rigged. The ship quickly broke up, and the number of spectators rapidly increased to over 3,000 when it was learnt that kegs of whisky were washing about in the shallows. Despite a strong presence of coastguards and customs officers, the entire foreshore was soon littered with drunken men and women, sleeping where they fell, making love, fighting over even more drink, or else just staggering around. Surprisingly, the first individual to come ashore in the basket was a negro seaman, then another male, then a female, followed by the captain! The female was a Mrs Irons, wife of the assistant steward on board, who was so fat that she stripped almost naked in order to get into the basket, and on reaching shore it took the combined efforts of three men to extricate her bulk.

The last ashore was the 2nd Mate, who reported that a married couple with a child remained on the stern (the only part of the vessel now above water), but had refused to leave. Some time later the man was seen to enter the basket with the child in his arms, but the traveller then broke, and they fell into the sea and drowned. Next day, twenty people were found dead on the foreshore, not one of whom were true victims of the wreck, for they had all died from alcoholic poisoning. The vessel's owners refused to bring any charges of theft against the 'wreckers', since they felt that such arrests would only take officials off the beach, in which case matters could only get worse. The total number of lives lost in the actual wreck was six, out of sixty-seven.

Two wreck incidents in the Solent, during 1875 and 1878, representing both ends of the scale regarding loss of life, were particularly tragic due to the circumstances. Her Majesty's Royal Yacht *Albert* left Trinity Pier, Cowes, on the Isle of Wight, on 18 August 1875 for a cruise. On board were Queen Victoria and other members of the royal family, then resident at Osborne. His Serene Highness Prince Leiningen was captain of the vessel, assisted by Captain Welch RN, acting as navigating officer. While steaming through Stokes Bay towards the Spit Buoy, the schooner *Mistletoe* appeared on the port bow of the royal yacht, then tacked right across her bow close hauled. Exactly who was at fault is difficult to determine, but in an age when steam most certainly *should* have given way to sail, in this case having the advantages of manoeuvrability and a maximum speed of fifteen knots, there seems little excuse for the resultant collision other than that the *Albert* was the royal yacht, and no doubt exercised a certain privilege. Having struck the schooner between her fore and main masts, burying her stem some 10ft into her hull, the steamship backed off and the *Mistletoe* sank, directly beneath the royal gaze. Navy divers were sent from HMS *Excellent*, at that time the RN Diving School, and the *Duke of Wellington*, who found the wreck intact and upright in 13 fathoms. The body of a Miss Peel was discovered beneath the main sail, and that of the master, Thomas Stoker, below decks. But no trace was found of the mate, Nathaniel Turner, the remainder of the crew having escaped at the moment of impact.

In contrast, the loss of the naval sail training ship *Eurydice* off Ventnor, Isle of Wight, on 24 March 1878, left the Royal Navy and the nation stunned. An old 26-gun, 6th-rate frigate, built at Portsmouth in 1843 and reduced to a training role in 1861, she was the second such frigate to bear the name. At the time of loss, all twenty-six of her old 32- and 12-pounder cannon had been replaced by four 64-pounder modern guns, used only for gunnery practice and drill. Her freeboard was therefore increased and her draught decreased, which may have contributed somewhat to her capsize. Throughout 1877 she cruised the English Channel, regularly passing Spithead and the Needles, as her crew of young seamen were welded into an efficient ship's company. That November the ship was ordered to the West Indies, and on 6 March 1878 left Bermuda for home. On Sunday 24 March they were off the south coast of the Isle of Wight, within two or three miles of Ventnor, heading east, with all canvas set, including studding sails. A severe squall from the north, accompanied by blinding snow, caught them unawares as it came at them from off the land, and even as the topmen were racing aloft to take in the royals and topsails, the captain ordered them back on deck for their own safety. As the full force of the squall struck them, Captain Marcus Augustus Stanley Hare ordered the main sheets and halyards cut to ease the strain, but she was thrown on her beam ends and never recovered. The sea poured in through the open lee ports, and in less than five minutes she went under. Ten to fifteen minutes later the squall had passed, the snow gone, and the wind dropped to a stiff breeze with sunlight sparkling on the waves. But the *Eurydice* was a total wreck. Off Sandown Bay, a little over 2 miles from shore, only the mastheads of the frigate showed above the surface in 11 fathoms.

The first vessel on the scene was the Padstow schooner *Emma* (Captain William Langworthy Jenkin), also caught in the squall but without incident. Hearing cries for help and aware of floating wreckage, they launched a boat and picked up four young men from the sea, and one from the rigging of the wreck. One of these died of exposure even before they could return to the *Emma*, and the remainder were in such a critical condition that the schooner made a dash for Ventnor with a flag at half-mast seeking assistance. Of the four survivors, Lieutenant Francis Tabor RN, 1st Lieutenant of the *Eurydice*, and Captain Ferrier RN, the latter returning home on leave from the West Indies, both succumbed before medical assistance was obtained, leaving but two survivors out of almost 350 on board. These were AB Benjamin Cuddiford and OS Sydney Fletcher, both of whom had managed to support themselves on lifebelts or jackets. Exactly how many persons were on board *Eurydice* is uncertain, but was assumed to be approximately 340. Apart from her sixteen commissioned officers and sixty-nine ship's company, she carried fifteen Royal Marines and an unspecified number of young seamen under training, as well as supernumaries. The latter included three prisoners awaiting court-martial from HMS *Rover* and her quartermaster, twelve marines from the Bermuda dockyard, two invalids from the hospital, three men from the *Argus* and a dockyard cook. Compared with the loss of the *Royal George* at Spithead in 1792, the widows of the dead were more fortunate in that they all received the equivalent of one year's service pay. After many weeks of work, the entire wreck of the *Eurydice* was raised, taken into Portsmouth and broken up.

Although the 1880s saw an incredible number of losses around the British Isles, the escalating annual total had peaked in 1876. In that one year, a total of 838 shipwrecks of all types occurred, of which 780 were sailing vessels and 58 steamships. During the previous decade the greatest number of losses took place during 1867, when the number reached 746; the awesome total for the period 1861–70 was 5,826 shipwrecks in the UK, with 8,105 lives lost. A great many casualties were caused along the coast of East Anglia by the severe gale of 29 October 1880. No less than thirty-six coasting vessels were driven ashore in the vicinity of Wells, and the first RNLI lifeboat there, the *Eliza Adams*, took the lives of eleven of her crew of thirteen when the so-called self-righting boat capsized, and failed to right itself due to wind pressure on her sail. With ten widows and twenty-seven orphans left in the town as a result of the accident, the most tragic aspect was the fact that the crew of the *Ocean Queen*, the Sunderland snow to whose assistance the lifeboat had been launched, waited aboard the wreck until the tide was low, then walked ashore! The third week of January 1881 saw an equally severe period of weather, and the reports of wrecks in the *Whitby Times* newspaper, echoed incidents the length of the east coast. It was the sight of burning tar-barrels at sea on 15 January, an international signal of distress in those days, that took the Whitby lifeboat, stationed at Upgang, a mile to the north of the town, to sea to investigate. Beaten by the fury of the gale and with the boat half full of water they returned, empty handed, as did the *Robert Whitworth*, another lifeboat of the National Society stationed at Whitby. The wreck proved to be the *Lumley* of South Shields, which went to pieces with the loss of all nine crew. On the 25th, two vessels went ashore in shallow water at Gorleston-on-Sea, Norfolk, one either side of the pier. The crew of one escaped, but those on board the *Corunna* of Whitby were to perish in front of thousands of onlookers. All attempts to reach the wreck by rocket apparatus failed, so the Gorleston lifeboat was launched, but became stuck on a sandbank due to tide being low. For over two hours, hundreds of people, up to their waists in water, tried to get the lifeboat afloat. But to no avail. As it became dark, everyone drifted home, leaving those aboard the wreck to their fate. Despite the fact that a woman and several sailors could be seen in the rigging, and their cries for help were plainly heard on the pier, it seems that nothing could be done, and all seven drowned. Meanwhile, the Clacton-on-Sea lifeboat, *Albert Edward*, was out on the Maplin Sand investigating reports of a wreck, when her crew found not one sailing vessel, but three others and a steamship!

The January of 1881 was equally tragic, with shipping on the coast of South Wales worst affected. An iron barque of London, the *Mirella,* went ashore between Lavernock Point and Penarth Head, along with the *Restless* of Salcombe, the *Pitching,* and five others. On West Cardiff flats, the Bristol Pilot Boat No 5, the ketch *Amazon* and four others were total wrecks, and in the vicinity of the Penarth lifeboat house were the *Wave*; *Elizabeth Diligence*; *Parkside*; *Jeanne Marie*; *Etta*; *Juan*; *Buckhurst*; *Miner*; *Georgina*; *Fanny June*; *Cyril*; *Achilles*; *Jeune Emilie*; *America* on One Fathom Bank near Cardiff, and elsewhere the *William*; *Admiral Cecill* and *White Eagle*.

The incidents are endless, such that it is impossible to determine the severity or impact of one compared to another. If any one wreck has to be chosen to end this chapter, then the *Stella* on the Casquets, in the Channel Isles, is as good as any other. It was about 6.30 am on Friday 31 March 1899 when Captain Winter of the passenger ferry steamship *Vera* sighted two small boats ahead, crowded with people all wearing lifejackets. As the word spread around the *Vera,* so her passengers crowded the rails to witness for themselves the recovery of survivors of some sea disaster, and only then did they learn they were from a sister ship of their own, namely the *Stella*. Both vessels belonged to the London & South-Western Railway Co, and were engaged in the Southampton–Channel Isles service. The *Stella,* of 1,059 tons gross, an iron steamship with a crew of forty-three, had left Southampton on 30 March with 174 passengers, bound for Guernsey. Fog was encountered off the islands, and she ran on to the Casquet Rocks at full speed. The rush of water indicated severe damage below the waterline, and all four ships' boats were launched and filled with a mixture of passengers and crew. As the last boat pulled clear, the steamer slipped back off the rocks, her bows went almost perpendicular, and she plunged beneath the surface, only eight minutes after striking. Those unable to get into a boat either clambered on top of a floating furniture van carried as deck cargo, or else made for the rocks. One of the boats was swept into the dangerous Race of Alderney, which runs between the island and the coast of France, and were adrift for almost two days. During that time six of the occupants died of exposure, despite the fact they were passed by several steamers, one as close as a quarter of a mile away, but no-one saw them. It was the keen eyesight of a coastguard at Ormonville La Hogue that led to their rescue by a French tug. Two other boats from the wreck were found by the Great Western steamer *Lynx*, which now brought the total rescued to 112, namely twenty-four crew and eighty-eight passengers. Other ships of the fleet joined in the search, including the *Honfleur* and *South Western*, the tug *Alert* and local boats. The *South Western* herself ran on a rock, and had to be beached on the coast of France, while the remainder searched the entire reef area, finding lifebelts, wreckage, two empty boats containing female clothing, money and jewellery and opera glasses, but no survivors. Bodies were in fact swept away by the tide, and weeks later the corpse of a Mr Collier, ex-mayor of Godalming, was picked up 70 miles away. When finally the search was abandoned, eighty-six passengers and nineteen crew were still missing.

7

THE PRICE OF WAR

1900–1919

It took the Admiralty an incredibly long time to learn to live with technology at the turn of the century. With the Royal Navy predominant still at the four corners of the world, its might not seriously challenged since Trafalgar, the majority of its senior officers were still obsessed with the old habits of sail and the ram bow, and were more concerned with 'spit-and-polish' than the fact that sailors were denied the opportunity to learn to shoot straight. With the triple expansion reciprocating engine only twenty-five years old, the quadruple version less than five, and the steam turbine only three, battleships were now capable of an incredible 16–20 knots. In many unfortunate accidents it was proven that the designers of warships had a lot to learn about stability, and that admirals and captains were not automatically capable of handling such powerful vessels, and the loss of a number of capital ships and thousands of men was to be the price. Although still fourteen years ahead, the demand that World War I was to place on both the Royal and Merchant Navies could not possibly have been foreseen, since the loss of shipping and men was on a scale never before experienced. In the meantime, both services slowly came to terms with smoke-blackened superstructures, steel decks instead of scrubbed wood, electric power, grubby engineers ranking equal with those on the bridge, radio communication, and other inventions.

At a time when shipbuilders such as Armstrong Whitworth

built warships and then offered the completed vessel for sale, this company informed the Admiralty on 12 December 1899, that two destroyers were available for purchase. Ships No 673/4 were not destroyers in the modern sense (that is, warships designed to destroy submarines), but rather torpedo-boat destroyers, light, fast craft intended solely for that function. No 674, later named HMS *Cobra*, was fitted with quadruple shafts, each carrying three propellers, driven by steam turbines. On trials, one such craft had achieved 29 knots, and HMS *Viper*, a sister ship, an incredible 35·5 knots. Unfortunately the latter became a total wreck off Alderney, in the Channel Isles, on 3 August 1901 in dense fog. Following acceptance into naval service, a lieutenant was chosen as her senior officer, and, accompanied by fifty crew, the first and last ship's company for the *Cobra* travelled to Newcastle to commission the ship and steam her round to Portsmouth. Her orders were to pass no closer than five miles off Flamborough Head, and to pass between the Outer Dowsing and Dudgeon, but outside the Gabard and Galloper Shoals. *Cobra*'s commanding officer was also instructed to sail at dawn, and anchor either off Great Yarmouth or Harwich for the night. The planned early start on 16 September was not possible, since not all the navigational equipment had arrived on board and her compasses had not been swung. It was therefore 5 pm before the *Cobra* cleared the mouth of the Tyne, and with a heavy sea on her starboard quarter and rolling heavily, her speed was reduced from 17 knots to 5. She steamed all night in these conditions, the craft being thrown about violently, but with improved conditions around dawn, her speed was again increased.

At 7 am on 17 September, the crew of the Outer Dowsing light-vessel were watching the approach of *Cobra*, noticing that she was 'plunging heavily', when she stopped, became enveloped in steam, and literally broke in two. The two sections drifted for a moment or two, then the stern sank, and the bow went away south on the tide. The chief engineer of the destroyer later reported feeling a sharp impact, followed only two or three minutes later by the complete fracture of the hull. Although a naval whaler, a 14ft dinghy and three collapsible Berthon boats were carried, the largest capsized when too many men clambered over the gunwhale, and the collapsibles could not be assembled, so only the dinghy with eight men aboard got clear. The number of survivors was increased to twelve as four more were hauled out of the water over the stern, and in a condition so cramped they could not even row, they managed to remain afloat in rough seas for eleven hours, before rescue by the SS *Harlington*. The sunken bow section of the *Cobra* was finally located and examined by a diver, but the stern was never found, and hence no proof exists as to whether the destroyer broke in two due to a design weakness, stress of weather, or as a result of having struck wreckage. SS *Oakwell*, a cargo vessel, reported steaming over floating timbers, possibly from a wreck, in a position 6 miles north-east of the Dudgeon Lightvessel, which could have caused the loss of the warship.

Although some twenty submarines of the Royal Navy have been lost or suffered serious accident in peacetime, since their acceptance into service in 1903, it was not imagined that one of these strange craft would be wrecked within less than a year. The first accident involved the submarine *A.1*, whilst engaged in fleet exercises in 1904. After conducting dummy attacks on the cruiser *Juno* near the Nab Tower, at the entrance to the Solent, the 165-ton submersible was returning to Haslar Creek, when her captain sighted the Union Castle liner *Berwick Castle* approaching. Exactly what happened will never be known with any certainty, but it is assumed that the *A.1*'s captain carried out a further dummy attack, got into a position such that he was rammed, and sank with loss of all hands. A combination of bad weather and inexperience in salvaging sunken submarines kept her on the bottom for five weeks, after which the wreck was raised, and towed back to the dockyard for examination. The accident highlighted a deficiency in submarine design, and from that day all such craft have been fitted with both a lower and upper hatch in the conning tower. Had the *A.1* been so fitted, having only the latter, when the *Berwick Castle* ploughed through her super-structure, a lower hatch would have maintained her water-tight integrity, and she would have survived. Returned to service after a complete refit, she survived until October 1913, when she sank off the Eddystone Reef, Devon, whilst on tow to the breaker's yard.

Despite the vast traffic in emigrants during the latter part of the nineteenth century, there were still some shipping companies making money from this trade in the early 1900s, which led to what has become known as 'the Great Rockall Disaster'. Without doubt the most isolated part of the British Isles is the island of Rockall, which lies 150 miles from St Kilda and 290 miles due west of Ross-shire in Scotland. It was not until the 1960s that it was officially annexed by HM Government, in order to extend the nation's territorial limits for offshore exploration, prior to which this uninhabited rock had no owner. Because of its shape, it has often been mistaken in the past for a ship under sail, and it is on record that a navy frigate once 'cleared for action' and gave chase! Although the island itself rises vertically out of the sea, shallow, dangerous reefs radiate from it for several miles, and it was upon one of these, known as Helen's Reef, that the Danish steamer *Norge* came to an untimely end on 28 June 1904. Owned by the United Steamship Co of Copenhagen and employed in the emigrant trade, she left Christiansund, Norway, for New York on 26 June, carrying a crew of sixty-eight and over 600 passengers. These were a polygenous collection of people, mostly Finns, Swedes and Russians, the latter fleeing from Poland in order to avoid military service in the Russo-Japanese war.

At 7.45 am on the 28th, the *Norge* drove straight over the top of one of the shallow reefs emanating from Rockall, and the dreadful tearing, screeching sound from below told its own story, the ship having literally torn out her bottom plates. Despite eight lifeboats and some rafts, their total carrying capacity was not nearly sufficient to rescue all aboard, even assuming they could all be safely launched. One boat overturned on entering the water, another was stove in against the ship's side in lowering, a third fell from the davits due to its overcrowding, but five managed to get clear. Twenty minutes after striking the reef, the *Norge* filled and sank, her upper deck still packed with humans. Those who could swim and hence jumped into the sea, were faced with the prospect of remaining afloat until rescued, or attempting to reach Rockall; those still on the wreck, of clutching floating wreckage to remain alive, or else being sucked under as the ship foundered. To avoid being swamped by the mass of people in the water, all of whom expected to be taken aboard the small boats despite the fact that they were already full, they had no choice but to row away from the scene. This brought a fearful death wail from the abandoned. Six days were to pass before the world knew of the disaster, and only then when the trawler *Salvia* reached Grimsay, in the Hebrides, with twenty-seven survivors.

Although the trawler had arrived on the scene by chance only six hours after the wreck, these twenty-seven were the only survivors in the water. The skipper reported 'a sea of wreckage and bodies supported by lifebelts or timbers, a spectacle too horrid to depict'. Rescue ships were despatched to the area, and for a time it was feared that only twenty-seven had survived out of 668. But then news was received of the lifeboats. One was picked up by the vessel *Energie*, who landed fifty-six survivors at Stornoway, another reached the Faroe's, but of the remainder, nothing was heard and it was assumed they had been swamped and sunk. Exactly how many survived is uncertain, but close on 600 lives were lost in that one wreck.

Throughout Devon's long history of shipwreck, which includes more than one county's fair share of men o' war, only the tiny island of Lundy, lying 12 miles off the north coast, well out into the Bristol Channel, can claim a 'modern' battleship amongst its marine victims. It was late in the afternoon of 29 May 1906 when a telegram was received at

Whitehall advising their Lordships that the five-year-old, 14,000 ton Duncan-class battleship *Montague* was stranded on the Shutter Reef, at the south-western corner of the island. Engaged in Fleet exercises, testing her new 'wireless tele-graphic signalling apparatus', her loss can be attributed directly to fog and faulty navigation. Finding the ship en-veloped in dense fog, and unwilling to anchor in a busy shipping channel, her commanding officer elected to move nearer to Lundy. At 2 pm, with 17 fathoms of water reported, her navigating officer calculated they were still 4 miles off-shore, yet twelve minutes later she was ashore and badly holed. If there can be any humour in such a situation, in this instance it was to be found amongst the landing party which scaled the high cliffs, and walked the length of Lundy to reach the northern lighthouse. It took the keeper some time to appreciate that his unexpected visitors thought that they were on the mainland of Devon, and that this was the Hart-land light. A heated argument then ensued, the young naval lieutenant being convinced he was right, and that the poor keeper was an idiot. The discussion came to an abrupt end when the local turned his back on him with the withering comment, 'Do you imagine I don't know *which* bloody light I'm keeping?'

The task of attempting to refloat the *Montague* was placed in the hands of the Liverpool Salvage Association and the very experienced Captain F. Young, but only in a secondary or advisory capacity to Admiral Sir A. K. Wilson RN. Though he was no doubt a brilliant career officer, unfor-tunately his knowledge of marine salvage was zero; and despite ordering battleships, cruisers, destroyers, auxiliaries and literally thousands of men to the scene, it was simply a case of 'too many cooks'. Slabs of heavy armour plating and her main armament were removed to make the wreck more buoyant, but salvage pumps were lost overboard or else fell down hatches, caissons broke adrift, wires and slings parted, and the hundreds of sailors achieved little but got in one another's way. Unfortunately history does not record Captain

Young's retort after the admiral seriously suggested that the battleship's interior should be filled with sheet cork, so that she could float up on the tide! With her upper deck now almost awash at high water, it was obvious to all that the fight was lost, and that the *Montague* was a total loss. Overnight the armada of supporting vessels departed, leaving her abandoned to the salvors and the Western Marine Co of Penzance, who removed her condensors, the remainder of the armament, tons of non-ferrous metal and naval stores. Six months later only a few rusting plates showed above the surface, and today nothing visible remains of this unfortunate incident, but on the seabed her frames and scattered plating are a grim reminder. The inevitable court-martial, held on board HMS *Victory* at Portsmouth, saw Captain Adair and Lt Dathan, the navigating officer, jointly facing the charge that they 'having by negligence or default, did hazard, strand or lose HM ship *Montague*'. Both officers were found guilty, receiving severe reprimands and being dismissed from their ship; additionally, the latter was deprived of two years' seniority in rank.

Since its inception in 1824 as the Royal National Institution for the Preservation of Life from Shipwreck, which became the Royal National Lifeboat Institution, the record for lives saved at any one incident remains with the 12,500-ton White Star Line's *Suevic*, wrecked on the Lizard during the night of 17 March 1907. Four local lifeboats between them rescued 456 passengers and crew, the Cadgwith boat saving 227, the Lizard boat 167, the Coverack 44 and the Porthleven 18 persons. Homeward bound from Australia with 141 crew and 382 passengers, plus one stowaway, her cargo was a valuable consignment of frozen meat, butter and copper bars. She called first at Plymouth; then, whilst on passage for Liverpool, went ashore on the Outer Cledges or Stags Reef at the Lizard in bad visibility. Following an underwater inspection by divers, it was decided that the after section of her hull from the forward boiler room bulkhead aft could be saved, and therefore the wreck was literally cut in two using explosives. With the damaged bow section left on the rocks to break up, the salvaged portion was towed away to Southampton, where it was eventually mated with a new bow unit built at Belfast. During World War I, the 'new' *Suevic* served as a troopship, being eventually sold to a Norwegian whaling company in 1929 and renamed *Skyttern*, and surviving as a factory vessel until the German occupation. On 1 April 1942, her crew scuttled the vessel in the Skagerrak, rather than let her fall into enemy hands.

The year 1908, and April in particular, was nothing short of disastrous for the Royal Navy, since in that month alone they lost three warships in three different incidents. Eighteen miles south of St Catherine's Point, on the Isle of Wight, HM Destroyer *Tiger* was engaged in night attack exercises on the Home Fleet on 2 April. Whilst running in for an attack, the torpedo boat flotilla got out of touch with each other, and in the ensuing confusion, the 400-ton *Tiger* cut across the bows of the cruiser *Berwick*, and was run down. Cut clean in two, the bow section immediately sank, but the remainder stayed afloat long enough for thirteen men to be rescued from the deck. A total of twenty-two were saved, but her Commanding Officer, Lieutenant W. E. Middleton, and twenty-seven others drowned. Twenty-three days later, on 25 April, the 2nd-class cruiser *Gladiator*, passing through the Needles Channel in the vicinity of the Isle of Wight again, collided off Yarmouth with the American liner *St Paul* during a blinding snowstorm. On passage from Portland to Portsmouth, the helm of the 5,750-ton warship was put to port when the liner was sighted ahead coming towards her. The *St Paul* also went to port, leaving both vessels well clear of each other on opposite courses, but then the liner's bow swung to starboard and she plunged her bow deep into the hull of the *Gladiator*, just abaft her forward funnel. At the time of the collision, the cruiser was proceeding at a cautious 9 knots, but the liner was making 16, a totally irresponsible speed in reduced visibility and a narrow shipping channel. Following the collision, the liner backed off, her engines going full astern, leaving the warship to flood. With steam pressure falling rapidly, and the vessel assuming an alarming list to starboard, the *Gladiator* was turned for the shore and beached 400 yards off the coast, near Black Rock buoy, under Fort Victoria. The death toll was surprisingly low, since out of a ship's company of 450 only one lieutenant and twenty-seven men were found to be missing. Of these, only three bodies were ever found. One of those missing, who had been picked up by a fishing craft, died later from exposure.

The salvage of the sunken cruiser presented a formidable task, since she lay on her starboard side, covering the 50ft-long gash in her hull, with her port side just above the surface. Not surprisingly, the contract was awarded to Captain F. W. Young of the Liverpool Salvage Association, whose first consideration, as with the *Montague*, was to remove as much armament and armour plating as possible. Off too came her funnels and ventilators, each hole being sealed and made watertight. Two tripods were erected on the port-side plating, from which heavy wires led off to powerful tugs. Seven massive pontoons, each 50ft long, were lashed alongside. Assisted by 280 tons of iron piled on her keel to act as a counterweight, five months after she sank the *Gladiator* came upright and was towed into Portsmouth. The salvage work cost the Admiralty £50,500; the wreck was sold to a shipbreaker for £15,125!

Only two days after the unfortunate *Gladiator* incident, a second destroyer was lost following collision near the Outer Gabbard Shoal, which lies 24 miles off Harwich. Fifteen ships of the Eastern Destroyer Flotilla were on exercises in the North Sea, when the 570 ton HMS *Gala* was struck by the cruiser *Attentive*. Its ram bow penetrated the smaller vessel's engine room and literally cut her in two. In the resultant confusion, with lights everywhere, and the noise of high-pressure steam escaping and men screaming, the cruiser swung away only to ram HM Destroyer *Ribble* as well. Fortunately it suffered only minor damage, but was forced to return to Sheerness for repairs. The bow section of the

Gala sank almost immediately, the stern remaining afloat long enough to enable the entire crew to be saved, apart from Eng Lieut Fletcher, who was trapped below. Although attempts were made to tow the stern half to shallow water, it filled and sank several miles offshore.

Although sail was in the early throes of decline during this period, and a further quarter century was to pass before the last of the 'giant' wind-powered ships gave way to steam, vessels such as the *Sovereign of the Seas*, *Pama*, *Penang*, *Padua*, *Viking*, *Pisagua* and *Preussen* were still world-famous. At the time of her loss in 1910, the latter was the largest five-masted, full-rigged sailing ship in the world. Launched at Geestermunde in 1902, for the German owner Laiez of Hamburg, she was of 4,765 registered tons, with an overall length of over 407ft. Shortly before midnight on 6 November 1910, she was headed down the English Channel under full sail, bound for West Africa and Iquique in Chili, via Cape Horn. She carried a general cargo valued at some £22,000, which included 100 pianos, a crew of forty-eight under Captain Nissen, and two passengers. About 8 miles off Newhaven, the Newhaven–Dieppe Channel steamer *Brighton* ran into her, bringing down the *Preussen*'s foremast and breaking off her bowsprit and jib-boom, as well as tearing a large hole in her bow plates. Having struck bow on, the steamer was less severely damaged, but had her deck swept almost clear, as the *Preussen*'s wire rigging and high bow tore away her foremast, forward funnel, and all the port-side lifeboats. To his credit, despite the responsibility of eighty passengers and the mail on board, the captain of the *Brighton* remained on the scene until forced by deteriorating weather conditions and a bad leak, to run for the shelter of Newhaven harbour. Events concerning the *Preussen* then assumed something of nightmare proportions for Captain Nissen. A tug sent to assist could not locate them; two anchors and 90 fathoms of chain on each were lost in East Bay, near Dungeness; tugs took her in tow, but the wires parted. Finally, with even the weather against them, since the gale blowing had now increased to force 8/9, the proud vessel went ashore in Fan Bay, near Dover, only 200 yards from the high cliffs.

Despite the presence of the Dover lifeboat, up to *ten* salvage tugs at any one time, and two rocket lines fired from the cliffs, lying across the wreck with which breeches buoys could be rigged, the Germans refused to abandon the vessel. Her captain left to talk to the ship's agent, but came ashore in a small boat, and then found himself unable to return. It was not until the late afternoon of 9 November that the crew and passengers finally left, having been in considerable distress for over forty-eight hours. Abandoned as a total loss, her owners placed a claim in the Admiralty Court for £74,000 compensation, against the London, Brighton and South Coast Railway Company, who admitted that the collision was the fault of the *Brighton*, but only £8,761 was paid over, being the limit of the Railway Companies liability to all claims.

Whereas in the previous incident, it was a steamship that brought about the loss of the giant *Preussen*, in March 1912 a similarly large full-rigged ship belonging to the same German company, actually sank a P&O liner off Beachy Head. Outward bound from Tilbury to Bombay, the crack RMS *Oceana* was carrying a general cargo, forty passengers, 220 crew and £747,110 in gold and silver bars, and gold specie, when the sharp bow of the *Pisagua* ploughed into her port side. The collision occurred at about 4 am on 16 March, with both the ship's chief and 2nd officers on the bridge, plus a Trinity House pilot. It seems they were all unaware of the sailing ship's starboard light, and the blue flares she was burning when it was obvious the vessels were too close, until it was too late to take any avoiding action. Of similar tonnage to the liner, and of steel construction, the nitrate-laden *Pisagua* tore a 45ft-long gash in the liner's hull, as well as smashing a whole line of davits and lifeboats. With her engine stopped, the *Oceana* wallowed in the swell, water pouring in as she listed more and more to starboard, but with all sail set, the *Pisagua* tore off into the darkness and vanished, although her foretop mast had come crashing down, and her entire bow was destroyed beyond belief.

Attempts were made to launch the liner's boats from the undamaged starboard side, but accident followed accident, and the final count of seven passengers and ten crew drowned could well have been worse, had not the cross-Channel steamer *Sussex* sighted her distress rockets, and gone alongside. Assisted by the Newhaven and Eastbourne lifeboats, the tug *Alert* and the collier *Queensgarth*, a total of 27 passengers and 187 crew were rescued. Taken in tow by the *Alert*, the liner slowly sank deeper and deeper, until off Eastbourne and within 2 miles of the Royal Sovereign lightvessel, she heeled over, her stern rose clear of the sea and she plunged to the bottom. Twenty minutes later, only her mast tops were visible above the surface. Once again, Captain Young was called in to organise the salvage, of first the bullion, and then if possible, the ship itself. The first box of gold was raised ten days after she sank, and subsequently almost all the money was recovered, but the wreck remains on the seabed to this day.

In the last twelve months of peace before World War I erupted, the Lizard headland in Cornwall, notorious for its hundreds of previous losses, claimed two more of this country's well-known full-riggers. The *Queen Margaret*, one of only two British-registered ships ever to carry three staysails, arrived off the Lizard at 4 am on 13 May 1913 from Sydney with her holds full of wheat. At first light, a colourful string of flags identified her to the watchkeepers in Lloyds Signal Station, who replied with the message that Captain Bousfield was to proceed to Limerick to discharge. The wind being only light, a tug was requested to help them clear the Land's End peninsula. It was whilst awaiting a reply from the owners, the ship in the meantime beating back and forth in front of the station, that the *Queen Margaret* impaled herself on the Maenheere rock, half a mile offshore. At low water she literally fell over, her four masts breaking off, and as her cargo saturated it swelled and burst out through her hull plating.

Only eighteen days later, the *Cromdale* went ashore close at hand, in fact so close to the land that her first distress rocket burst in front of the coastguard station, giving the duty officer, totally unaware that the wreck had taken place, the shock of his life! She went ashore a little to the east of Bass Point in dense fog, and looked a fine sight next day, with all her sails set, and hanging limp in the damp air. The *Queen Margaret* was sold as a wreck for £50, the *Cromdale* for £41; a week later a full gale smashed the latter to pieces.

It was 4 August 1914 when ships of the Royal Navy were ordered to commence hostilities against German vessels, and fortunately the magnitude of shipping losses and human life which lay ahead was totally unpredictable. Although the greater percentage of losses at sea were attributable to what is best described as 'submarine warfare', there was still the annual toll of conventional marine casualties, aggravated as the war progressed by the extinguishing of shore beacons, the civilian blackout and dimmed lights aboard ships, zig-zag steaming in convoys, and less professional crews. No statistics exist showing exactly how many ships went to the bottom in UK waters, but world wide, between 1 July 1914 and 31 December 1918, 3,781 British registered merchantmen alone were destroyed, plus 915 additional marine casualties over the period. The number of lives which were lost in these incidents was an appalling 21,886. Ironically, before either a British warship or merchantman fell victim to torpedo, bomb or mine, the German submarine *U-15* was rammed and sunk by the light cruiser HMS *Birmingham*, between Scapa Flow and Fair Isle, on 9 August 1914. However, the enemy got its revenge a month later when on 3 September *U-21* fired a single torpedo at the light cruiser *Pathfinder*, when close to the Isle of May. This detonated her main magazine and within four minutes of the explosion she had gone under, the first occasion in modern warfare that a submarine had sunk a warship. The first merchant ship lost in the war in these waters was the British-owned SS *Runo*, mined 22 miles off the Tyne on 5 September, and the SS *Cambank*, on 20 February 1915—the first to be torpedoed, going down some ten miles east of Point Lynas.

In those early days, possibly the wreck of the hospital ship SS *Rohilla* on the coast of Yorkshire on 30 October did more to promote bad feeling against Germany than anything else that year. Belonging to the British India Steam Navigation Co, the *Rohilla*, once a famous troop and passenger vessel, had been taken into naval service as an auxiliary, and converted into a floating hospital. She struck a mine in the North Sea off Northumberland, and went ashore on the south edge of the Yellow Sand, amongst a mass of rocks near Saltwick, four miles south of Morpeth. Unable to render assistance from seaward due to the difficult approach, the crew of the Whitby lifeboat hauled their craft for about $\frac{3}{4}$ mile over sand and rocks, before launching opposite the wreck. Of the 229 crew and nurses aboard the *Rohilla*, eighty-five were killed.

Warlike activities excepted, internal explosion is an uncommon cause of a ship being lost, but such was the fate of HM Battleship *Bulwark* at Sheerness, Kent, on 26 November that same year. Lying quietly at anchor in Kethole Reach, between Port Victoria and Stangate Creek, she was suddenly overwhelmed by the explosion of her magazine. Lighters alongside had been discharging coal and ammunition, when without warning the ship was enveloped in a sheet of flame, followed by a thunderous shock wave and a huge cloud of smoke. Two minutes later, when the smoke had cleared, nothing of the battleship remained, except for floating wreckage and the dead. To this day the accident remains a mystery, but considering similar accidents yet to come, such as the explosion that sank the *Natal* in Cromarty Firth on New Year's Eve, 1915; the *Vanguard* at Scapa in 1917, and the *Glatton* in Dover harbour the following year, sabotage was considered the most likely cause. A less-well-known casualty of that first year of the war has been described in a recently published book as *The Other Titanic*. Designed and built for the Transatlantic route, to carry 2,000 passengers and 394 crew, the 30,000-ton White Star liner *Oceanic* was even more luxurious, although a little smaller than, her sister ship the *Titanic*. In August 1914, the *Oceanic* entered Southampton as a liner, and left as the armed merchant cruiser HMS *Oceanic*, but with a chain of command that was doomed to failure, and eventually contributed to the loss of the ship. Captain Henry Smith had been Master of the *Oceanic* for two years prior to the outbreak of war, but overall charge of the ship was placed in the hands of Captain William Slayter RN, with the result that the vessel had two 'captains', and virtually two crews, being Royal and Merchant Navy factions. She survived exactly two weeks, running ashore on Hoevdi Grund, south-east of the island of Foula, near Shetland, due to a gross error of navigation and a countermanding of orders. She broke her back on the reef and became a total loss, and the whole episode can best be described as a 'comedy of errors'. No wonder the crew of the *Oceanic* became known amongst the Fleet as the 'Muckle Flugga Hussars'!

In conventional war it is an unfortunate but acceptable risk that ships and men will be lost due to enemy action, but to lose them needlessly is unthinkable; to lose them to your own side is catastrophic. In the final traumatic twelve months of World War I, a routine exercise operation taking place in the North Sea turned into a nightmare, known sardonically ever since as 'The Battle of May Island'. It was 1 February 1918 when the British Grand Fleet, commanded by Admiral Beatty, sailed for Operation ECI, a force consisting of some thirty warships from battleships down to submarines. The latter were all '*K*' class boats, which had entered service in 1916 as a bold, imaginative, but disastrous development of the submersible. With a combination of steam turbines, electric motors and diesel engines as main propulsion units alone (a total of seven units in all), the complications of control, isolation, cooling, ventilation and fuel were unreasonable for a surface vessel, let alone a 340ft-long submarine. Hence the '*K*' class submarines were detested by their crews, and definitely considered unlucky, and for good reason. There had been far too many accidents already.

As the fleet slipped down the Firth of Forth, in the vicinity of May Island, from whence the incident derived its name, *K-14* apparently sighted some minesweepers in her path, and altered course to avoid them only to find her steering jammed. In the meantime, *K-22*, the last astern in the formation, having lost sight of the dim blue stern light of *K-12*, spotted a red navigational light to starboard, turned towards it and rammed *K-14*. Astern of them both, the battle-cruiser *Inflexible* bore down on *K-22*, struck her a tremendous blow that bent 30ft of her already-damaged bow at right angles to the hull. In passing she also tore off the submarine's ballast and fuel tanks, then swept majestically off into the darkness, her officers and crew completely ignorant of the collision. In an attempt to sort themselves out, *K-17* was run down by the cruiser *Fearless*, steaming at 21 knots, which inflicted such damage that this submarine eventually sank in 162ft of water. *K-12* nearly joined her luckless sister ship when the battle cruiser *Australia* almost ran her down, missing her bow by inches.

Close to the spot where the *K-17* had sunk, *K-6* plunged her sharp bow into the *K-4*, slicing deep into her pressure hull. For a while both craft lay locked together, despite *K-6*'s frantic attempts to free itself, her engines racing at full-astern and all ballast tanks blown. *K-4* then started to sink, taking the other vessel with it, but at the last minute *K-6* broke free, and literally bounced back to the surface, the other vessel sinking to destruction. The entire fleet was now in confusion, full navigational lights were ordered and searchlights swept the surface, it being generally assumed that they had been attacked by U-Boats. Following on behind the smaller ships were the battleships, which ploughed through the surfaced submarine flotilla, fortunately without incident, although two of them missed *K-3* by 'the thickness of her steel hull plating'. It was the escorting destroyers that wrought the final touch of havoc, when all ten of them tore through the area where the submarines lay, running down the survivors from

K-17 as they floated on the surface, awaiting rescue by *K-7* which was slowly edging in amongst them. Her deck party, all volunteers, were stripped off ready to enter the water to help their fellow submariners, but were washed off the deck casing by the destroyer's wake, and they too had to be rescued. Never in the history of the Royal Navy had there been such an unfortunate, expensive, appalling two hours of accidents.

What ranks as the most momentous shipwreck incident in history, not only around the British Isles but in the world, began on 21 November 1918, when at 9.40 am the German High Seas Fleet, steaming in perfect formation, passed between two columns of Allied warships waiting in double line ahead, and so passed into internment. Headed by the battleship *Friedrich Der Grosse*, followed by eight other battleships, five battle-cruisers, eight light cruisers and forty-nine destroyers—a total of seventy-one warships—they completed the formal rituals of surrender and by 27 November were at anchor in Scapa Flow, awaiting a decision as to their fate. Other German ships arrived, and by 13 December their number had risen to seventy-four, but with only a token maintenance party of some 1,800 officers and men, the remainder of the crews having been repatriated back to Germany.

The situation for the remaining members of the once proud German navy was intolerable—total ignominy and degradation, the object of curiosity to boatloads of sightseers. They hated every minute of this false 'captivity', and eventually the discontent erupted into drunkenness and open mutiny. Although the Peace Terms concerning the fleet had been signed in June 1918, some six months earlier, there was the inevitable bickering between the Allied nations as to its disposal. Great Britain wanted the entire fleet destroyed and reduced to scrap metal. But other nations, France in particular, with smaller fleets than this country, saw this as an opportunity to adjust the balance of seapower at no expense to their government, and demanded that they be shared out. On 20

June 1919, after seven months of complete idleness and humiliation and the Allies no nearer to an agreeable solution, the secret plans of Von Reuter were put into action. This called for the scuttling of the entire fleet 'if the English try to take us by force, or if a special order comes from me', (those were his exact words). At 11 am that day, a special two-pennant signal appeared at the yardarm of the light cruiser *Emden*, and was acknowledged by each of the German ships present. Since nothing untoward happened immediately, no suspicion was aroused amongst the British guard ships, and this country remained in complete ignorance of what was about to happen. The following day, 21 June, all the British fleet left Scapa apart from one destroyer, some drifters and a Depot ship.

The 'secret' signal ordered the Germans to 'sink all ships immediately', and on its second showing, sink them they did, and very efficiently! Not only did they open the sea cocks, but had had time to ensure that every watertight door was left open, every scuttle and porthole, hatchway, ventilator—in fact any opening. To ensure that any salvage would be difficult—if not impossible, they bent, disconnected or broke every connecting rod associated with bilge and pumping valves. Some of the warships settled down gracefully, upright, and with masts and funnels showing; others rolled over and capsized, some sank in shallow water, others in over 180ft. Some drifted around and stranded in shallow water, some did not sink at all. In fact, one battleship, three cruisers and eighteen destroyers remained intact and afloat, but fifty-two ships lay wrecked between the islands of Rija and Fara, or around Cava. The majority of these were salvaged over the years, but several of the deep wrecks remain, and are being worked to this day, over sixty years later. The Germans were elated, the Allies disgruntled, and the British furious at what they called this 'act of treachery'. Whatever it was, it has gone down in history as an appalling act of destruction.

8

WATERS OF WIDE EXPANSE AND FREE OF DANGERS!

1920–1979

The destruction of some 9,412,000 tons of British shipping alone, between 1 July 1914 and 31 December 1918, left those vessels that survived at a premium. For many years following World War I, there was renewed interest in sailing ships, which were attractive economically. It is therefore fitting that the first shipwreck in this chapter concerns an incident often recalled on the relevant part of the Yorkshire coast, as 'the schooner that would not die'. The vessel in question was the 1,500-ton, five-masted Canadian *Cap Palos*. Her notoriety was achieved following a series of events, commencing on 24 October 1919, which did not end until a year later. She was built on the Canadian Pacific coast at Vancouver for the French government, but on cessation of hostilities in 1918 they declined to take delivery, so her builders ran the vessel for themselves. Her maiden voyage began on 24 March 1919, and she arrived at Immingham, Lincolnshire, on 23 August, the passage protracted by a complete breakdown of her auxiliary engine. Repairs were arranged at Hartlepool, and the *Cap Palos* left under tow of the tug *Symbol* on 21 October, to be joined off Flamborough Head by a second, the *Cabal*. Three days later, both tugs went ashore off Ness Point, in Robin Hood's Bay, and but for swift action by the schooner's captain in slipping the tow line, the *Cap Palos* might well have been wrecked on the spot. Despite a strong onshore north-easter, the sailing ship managed to claw her way offshore where she anchored, but she dragged, and was soon back in shallow water, with her keel bumping on the bottom. Both tugs managed to get afloat again at high water, but seemingly wanted nothing further to do with the schooner, and steamed off, leaving the local lifeboat to render whatever assistance it could. Of the fourteen men aboard the *Cap Palos*, only five elected to leave, but as the gale intensified and the sea drove the wreck further on to the rocks, six more abandoned her using their own boat, leaving the Robin Hood's Bay lifeboat to rescue the master and two mates. Stranded and deserted, it was assumed the winter's gales would quickly tear her to pieces. But twelve months passed, and she remained intact.

A channel was finally blasted through the rocks, and on 1 October 1920, the *Cap Palos* was again afloat, under tow first for Whitby Roads, and then Blythe, where she was to be dry-docked. Outside Whitby she broke adrift in a gale and disappeared out to sea, chased by the Whitby lifeboat, which covered 18 miles before an opportunity presented itself to go alongside, and rescue the seventeen-man salvage crew. The last person to leave the ship was Captain Tennant, carrying the ship's cat! Left to drift around, the schooner slowly filled and settled lower in the water, until all that could be seen was a waterlogged hulk. It was a local trawler that eventually got it in tow, and brought the wreck ashore. Eventually, she broke in two, 2 miles north-east of Scarborough castle. Her stern half, which remained afloat, was towed into Cornelian Bay, and broken up, but the remainder sank.

1925 echoed the tragi-comic record of the British 'K' class submarines, which persisted in service up until 1932. In June 1918, in order to demonstrate their faith in the class, Britain ordered six more, the vessels to be numbered *K-23* to *K-28*. These made up for the losses, *K-19* to *21* inclusive having been converted into 'M' class submarine dreadnoughts. The original idea stemmed from Lord Fisher, who believed that a submarine mounting a single 12in gun was the ultimate weapon, particularly since British torpedoes at that time were notorious for every conceivable manoeuvre except sinking enemy ships. Frightened by the prospect of the Germans constructing a similar class of monitor, which could make a nonsense of the 'security' of the Scapa Flow anchorage, all work on *M-1* ceased, and covered by tarpaulins she remained untouched for almost a year. The pressures of war caused work to recommence in 1918, and by the June *M-1* was commissioned and in service. Ironically, instead of being used on the German North Sea coast, she was sent into the Mediterranean, and never fired a shot in anger. By the early 1920s, *M-1*, *2* and *3* were all in service as big gun 'mutton-boats' (as they were known), but the fleet never forgot that they all had '*K*' class keels. On 10 January 1924, the battleship *Resolution* rammed and sank the *L-24* submarine on exercises off Portland Bill, and the loss of forty-three men shocked the nation. But worse was to follow.

Early November 1925 saw the submarine tenders *Maidstone*, *Alecto* and *Ross*, plus submarines *M-1*, *M-3*, *L-17*, *22* and *23* entering Plymouth, prior to exercises. They departed on the 11th, *M-1* commanded by Lieutenant Commander A. Carrie, carrying a crew of sixty-eight. She dived at a position given as 15 miles south of Start Point, Devon, and was never seen again. Strenuous efforts were made to locate her, but a depth of some 250ft discouraged the use of conventional 'standard' flexible diving gear. The German Kiel National Salvage Co, Messrs Neufelde & Kulbuke, sent over one of their armoured deep-diving suits, and several dives were made, but nothing was found. Ten days later, the Swedish cargo vessel *Vidar* arrived at Kiel, to announce that she had struck a submerged object 15 miles off Start Point at 7.48 am on 12 November, the day the *M-1* had gone missing. A close scientific examination of her bent stem and buckled plates indicated collision with a metal object, painted a grey/green, and of a paint type identical to that used by the Admiralty on '*M*' class submarines. The search for the wreck continued until 9 December, when it was officially abandoned. The wreck has in fact never been found, despite claims in recent years to the contrary. The accident prompted a national outcry, it being the fourth such disaster since the war, in which a total of four submarines and 193 men had been lost.

Merchant ship losses continued, of course, summer and winter alike, with only a small reduction in the annual total. In 1926, for example, January saw the 211-ton auxiliary wooden schooner *Maggie A* sunk 8 miles north of Bude, Cornwall; the 227-ton iron steam trawler *Downie Hills* lost off Fifeness; the *Risoy*, a Norwegian schooner of 383 tons, which foundered in the North Sea; and a large Greek steamer, the *Eleftherios M. Tricoglu*, 2,633 tons, stranded and wrecked near Arranmore Island, Co Donegal. The total for the year was eighteen, discounting anything smaller than 100 tons. Little mention has been made of the British Lifeboat service, which has contributed to the saving of so many lives from shipwreck since its inception. That the service is a voluntary organisation never ceases to surprise foreigners, and that men will take the appalling risks they do for little or no reward beyond their comprehension. There have of course been a great many lifeboat disasters, when the rescuers become the victims, and in which an entire boatfull of men lost their lives for others.

One such incident at Rye, in Kent, during 1928, was brought about by a call for help from the Latvian steamer *Alice*, of Riga. It was 6.30 am on 15 November, during one of the worst gales remembered on that coast, that news came from the coastguards that a steamer was in distress, drifting helpless 8 miles off Dungeness. The manhandling of the boat out of its shed and to the slipway took the efforts of almost the entire male population of the village, and those left ashore no doubt feared for their companions' safety as they disappeared from sight in the driving rain. Exactly five minutes after launch, a further message was received that the crew of the *Alice* had been rescued by another steamship, but with no radio aboard, and unable to hear the recall maroon over the noise of the gale, the lifeboat continued. They remained at sea for four hours, searching in vain, then returned under sail. Just outside the harbour mouth, the Liverpool-type, non-self-righting boat was thrown end over end by a following sea, capsized, and threw its crew into the breakers.

There was absolutely nothing the onlookers could do but wait for the sea to bring in its gruesome cargo. First the lifeboat itself came ashore, bringing with it six entangled bodies; nine more floated in at intervals of up to three days. Three months then elapsed before the sixteenth was found, but nothing of John Hird was ever seen. All seventeen of the Rye lifeboat's No 1 crew died in that tragedy, and the effect on individual families and such a small community was heartbreaking. Herbert Head, the coxswain, had his two sons with him; the bowman, H. Cutting, his two brothers; three brothers from the Pope family were present, William and Leslie Clark were also brothers, and Maurice and Arthur Downey were cousins. Shocked and distressed by the accident, possibly the worst in the lifeboat service for many years, over £35,000 was collected by public subscription to assist the dependents. A memorial stone of Manx granite can still be seen at the harbour, and a stained glass window in Winchelsea church reminds each generation of the sacrifice. A tribute to the courage of the men of Rye was paid by HRH Edward, Prince of Wales, and President of the RNLI, in 1929, when he spoke at the annual general meeting held in Edinburgh:

> The Rye lifeboat crew have carried on the traditions of a service which, like every fighting service, has always involved the risk of the supreme sacrifice. Such men gave their lives for the common cause, and in so doing earn for themselves the praise that grows not old. Such tragedies are an inseparable part of the great enduring drama of the sea, and lend to the lives and death of the lifeboatmen an element of the sublime.

As with the lifeboat service, men other than those that serve aboard conventional ships, risk their lives for others, which must include Trinity House vessels, also subject to shipwreck. In February and March 1929, fog was the predominant feature of the weather throughout Kent, which persisted like a blanket for weeks, and the noise of foghorns, rattles, ships' bells and maroons offshore was unbelievable. It also brought serious accidents to two of the four light-vessels that guard the Goodwin Sands. It was almost noon on 24 February, but so dark it seemed like early morning, when the 7,885-ton German SS *Oliva* appeared out of the fog at full speed, and crashed headlong into the South Goodwin vessel. Fortunately no lives were lost, but less than four weeks later, the *Gull* lightship was also rammed and sunk, drowning its master, Captain Williams. It was the Ellerman liner *City of York*, 7,834 tons, that loomed out of the murk, going much too fast, and cut the lightship in two. Her bow sliced open the bunkroom, and the seven men asleep below woke up to find themselves swimming in a cold sea. But the master went to the bottom, trapped in his cabin, and divers had to recover the body.

The 1930s, which culminated in Great Britain again at war with Germany, began with news of the tragic loss of HM Submarine *M-2*, sister ship of the ill-fated *M-1*, now one of only two 'K' class designs remaining. All three 'M' class boats had originally mounted a single large gun each, but following the accident off Start Point in 1925, *M-2* had been converted to a seaplane carrier and *M-3* to a mine-layer. On 26 January 1932, *M-2* left Portland naval base, accompanied by the tender/drifter *Titania*, other vessels of the 6th Submarine Flotilla, and *L-67* and *71*. At 10 am Lieutenant Commander Leathes of *M-2* signalled his intention to dive, but failed to surface by 4.15 pm as arranged. By late evening a small fleet was engaged in the hunt, but Lyme Bay is littered with sunken ships, and has even been called 'The Bay of a Thousand Wrecks'. A report was then received that the captain of the SS *Tynesider* had actually seen the *M-2* sinking rapidly *by the stern*, $2\frac{1}{2}$ miles from shore, 8 miles from Portland Bill. It was 3 February before the *M-2* was found, 5·8 miles from the Bill, lying in 108ft of water, with her double hangar doors, upper conning tower, engine room and after-crew deck-hatches open to the sea. Salvage operations proceeded, hatches were sealed with cement, air injection valves fitted and lifting pontoons positioned, but after endless problems, bad weather, and some near-fatal accidents, salvage was abandoned on 8 December. It is interesting to note that the sum expended on the salvage work was about £15,000, which by present-day standards would be worth almost £600,000!

As war clouds gathered over Europe in 1936, news was received at Lloyds that one of the best known sailing ships in the world, the *Herzogin Cecilie*, had been wrecked on the south coast, in Devon. The winner of many long-distance grain races, and cadet ship for the Norddeutscher Lloyd Line until the commencement of World War I, *Herzogin Cecilie* was the last big four-masted barque to be wrecked in the South West. Known affectionately as the 'Old Duchess' (being a reference to her figurehead, a likeness of the Duchess Cecilie, daughter of the Duke of Oldenbourg), she maintained her reputation to the very end. She reached Falmouth from Australia in eighty-six days on her last passage, more than a week ahead of the *Pommern*, her nearest rival. Two days were spent at Falmouth, waiting for orders, then she sailed for Ipswich on 24 April, before her competitor had appeared off the Scillies. She sailed at 8.20 pm, cleared St Anthony Head and set course up Channel. At 4 am on the 25th, 10 miles out of dead reckoning and enveloped in fog, she stranded on the Hamstone rock, near Salcombe, almost on top of the rusting plates of the tea clipper *Halloween*, lost in 1887. The Salcombe lifeboat went to the wreck, and took off twenty-two of the crew, leaving only Captain Sven Eriksson, his wife Pamela, two mates and four seamen aboard. She lay on the rocks for seven whole weeks, an object of great interest to the thousands of sightseers, most of whom would never again see the wreck of a sailing ship. It was agreed that successful salvage was almost guaranteed, her hull having received little damage. But the rotting cargo, which gave off an appalling smell, caused the Salcombe harbour authority to refuse her entry, due to fears of extensive pollution of the local beaches. Refloated on 19 June, she was then beached in Starehole Bay, which seemingly had a safe, sandy bottom, after which a gang of volunteers began to shovel out some 3,500 tons of rotten grain into barges. Unfortunately, she settled too deep into the sandy bottom, sat on top of a hidden reef, and during a gale on 18 July, broke her back. Had the weather only remained settled for a further seven days, the remaining 1,500 tons of cargo would have been removed, the *Herzogin Cecilie* would have been pumped out, the leaks stopped, and she could have been saved.

The rocket life-saving apparatus had of course progressed a long way since Captain Manby and Henry Trengrouse gave it their attention in the early 1800s. The invention has been responsible for the saving of countless lives, and its success brought the Board of Trade Wreck Service Shield to Wales for the first time, in 1937. Burnham radio station was first to pick up the SOS message when the trawler *Roche Castle* signalled that she had gone ashore 10 miles west of Mumbles, during the night of 10 January. The Mumbles lifeboat was launched, but in appalling sea conditions she was helpless, and was forced to return. In the meantime a cliff search was instigated, and the wreck located under Paviland cliff, but the position was such that the Rhossili LSA Company had to manhandle their equipment over half a mile of rough ground. The first rocket fired took a line straight across the wreck, the crew of which hauled across the 'whip' and made fast to the top of the mast, but no attempt was made to come ashore. Her captain still hoped she would refloat herself on the flood tide, but as the water rose, she rolled over on her port side, and became half covered. By now, the crew of the *Roche Castle* were keen to leave, especially when whole seas began to break over the wreck, and to save time, two men at a time used the breeches buoy, instead of one. The first two climbed on, straddled the chair, and began the perilous journey to the clifftop. For a moment the hawser went slack as the wreck rolled, then snapped taut, catapulting one of the two men from off the buoy and into the boiling surf, where he was crushed to death between the rocks and the trawler's side. Those who followed were one moment high in the air, the next completely submerged. But the line held, and ten men reached safety in forty-five minutes.

The year 1939 was spectacular as regards shipwrecks, with incidents ranging in location from the Goodwin Sands to Scapa Flow, including the loss of a great many merchant ships, another British submarine, and the first major warship loss in British waters during World War II. HM Submarine *Thetis*, launched from Cammell Laird's Birkenhead yard in December 1936, was completed and commissioned on 4 March 1939, and sailed for her diving trials in Liverpool Bay on 1 June with 103 persons on board. Normally her complement would have been sixty-five officers and ratings, but because of the occasion she carried additional submarine officers, engineers, Admiralty officials and several representatives of the builders. A tug escorted the submarine to sea, its purpose being to take off some of the superfluous personnel before trials commenced, and to keep surface craft clear of the area. 38 miles out of Liverpool, and 15 miles north of the Great Orme Head, Llandudno, *Thetis* signalled that she was submerging for three hours. It took almost an hour to get her under for that first dive, then she disappeared beneath the surface quickly—too quickly in fact, at least for the limited experience of Lt Coltart, the junior liaison officer aboard the tug *Grebecock*. He was also concerned that Lieutenant Commander Bolus, commanding officer of the *Thetis*, had proceeded with the trials with numbers grossly in excess of her normal complement, which meant that in the event of an accident, the air supply would not last so long.

Although the details were not known till long after the *Thetis* had been salvaged and examined in dry dock, she had in fact dived with the outer door of No 5 torpedo tube open. Full of water, the additional weight made the craft bow heavy. Not appreciating that the tube was flooded, the 'tell-tale' indicator hole being blocked with paint, one of the officers opened the inner door. This caused her bow compartments to flood, and she sank to the bottom in 160ft. Although her stern showed clear of the surface for a time, it was impossible to open inspection covers in the hull, or to cut through, to save the men. Only four escaped, using DSEA (Davis Submarine Escape Apparatus); the remainder died inside the wreck.

Possibly one of the most remarkable coincidences in shipwreck history, two large steamships bearing the same name, belonging to the same shipping company, on the same voyage, were wrecked within less than a mile of each other on the Goodwin Sands—but thirty years apart! The first *Mahratta* was wrecked on 9 April 1909, on passage from Calcutta to London with passengers and a general cargo. On 6 October 1939, the second ship of the same name, belonging to the Brocklebank Line and having left Calcutta for London (with ninety crew, seventeen passengers, and 10,000 tons of assorted tea, jute, rubber and rice), stranded in Trinity Bay, close to the Fork Spit.

Although the aircraft carrier *Courageous*, torpedoed by a U-Boat west of Ireland on 17 September 1939, was the first major warship loss of World War II, it was the sinking of the battleship *Royal Oak* on 14 October the same year, that stunned the British public, and brought home the renewed horror of war. Throughout the entire period 1914–18, Scapa Flow had enjoyed complete sanctity, an impregnable haven for the mighty warships of the Grand and Home Fleets, vulnerable perhaps only to an attack from the air. With the declaration of war in 1939 only a month old, Admiral Doenitz, Hitler's *Grossadmiral*, had already conceived a plan to destroy one or more capital ships within Scapa by sending in a submarine. His choice of boat was *U-47*, its commanding officer Kapitanleutnant Gunter Prien. At 1.04 am on Saturday 14 October, Prien sent three electric torpedoes against the 29,000 ton *Royal Oak*, lying quietly at anchor, only one of which found its target. Three more were fired, each of which exploded against the battleship's starboard side, causing her to roll over and sink, taking 833 of her crew to their death. To this day, the *Royal Oak* remains where she sank, in 115ft, lying on her beam ends, unsalvaged apart from all four bronze propellers, which were cut off by the salvage vessel *Salvestor* in 1947. Even the massive ship's bell remains on the bottom, lying just clear of the wreck, on a sandy bottom, exactly where it was found by divers engaged in making a film during 1979.

One of the most remarkable accounts of German mine warfare and their success in sinking ships was an incident in which one mine caused the loss of three ships, over a period of eleven days. It all began on 3 November 1939, when the 11,108-ton Danish motor vessel *Canada* struck a moored mine, 2 miles east of Holmpton, north of Spurn Point, on the Yorkshire coast. The resultant explosion blew a hole in No 2 hold, and a day later she sank, a total loss. One week after, the 1,289-ton SS *Dryburgh* ran over the wreck of the *Canada*, was pulled clear but capsized, and became victim number two. Less than a further twenty-four hours had elapsed when the Humber lifeboat was at sea, assisting the SS *Fireglow*, a vessel of 1,261 tons, owned by the Gas, Light and Coke Co; she stranded on top of the *Canada* but pulled clear—unlike the Greek *Georgios*, 2,216 tons, which tore open her bottom plates on the wreck, and became the third victim when she sank a short distance away.

The official tonnage of shipping lost between 3 September 1939 and 2 September 1945 owing to enemy action, does not specify particular areas, so the numbers or tonnage of losses around the British Isles cannot be stated. What can be said is that the Royal Navy lost 1,503 ships, representing 959,757 tons (displacement), and the Merchant Navy 4,786 ships, equal to 21,194,000 tons (gross). Since coverage of even a small percentage of this vast number of losses would require a volume of its own, two incidents have been chosen at random, which add a degree of variation to the overall picture.

In 1944, after loading a cargo of aerial bombs and other munitions at Hog Island, Philadelphia, USA, the American Liberty ship *Richard Montgomery* sailed in convoy for the Thames, arriving on 20 August. The King's Harbourmaster allocated the ship an anchorage off the North End of Sheerness Middle Sand Shoal, where she lay in only 33ft of water, and since she drew 31ft, she grounded at low tide, and broke her back. Removal of her explosive cargo was not only of national importance, but was necessary because of the hazard it represented to the civilian population of Sheerness and its neighbouring dockyard. Work commenced on 23 August, and by the time she was abandoned, Nos 4 and 5 holds had been cleared, but little else. To this day, an estimated 3,553 gross tons of ordnance remains in the wreck, which settles deeper and deeper with each passing tide. Having been left alone these past thirty-six years, it is probably best left that way. To this day, her three masts still show, reminding us of the danger below.

Extinguishing navigational beacons and shore lights was a necessary precaution around the coast during the war years, which in some cases served to confuse our Allies more than the enemy! An unfortunate series of losses on the Goodwin Sands was brought about by the contents of a printed instruction, issued by the American authorities, as guidance to their captains regarding the use of pilots. It read:

> Numerous cases have been observed where pilots have been employed by ship masters at great expense, and without prior authority for waters such as the English Channel . . . employment of pilots for such waters is considered unnecessary . . . the subject waters are of wide expanse and relatively free of dangers . . . therefore the employment of pilots for these waters is disapproved.

One cannot help wonder if the Assistant Deputy Administrator for Ship Operations, G. H. Hembold, who was responsible for those instructions, was aware that the Goodwins had already claimed over 1,500 ships. As a direct consequence, two US ships stranded in 1945. Both of these were saved, but over the next two years the *Luray Victory*, *Helena Modjeska*, *North Eastern Victory*, *Ira* and *Fort Vermillion* all went ashore on the southern Goodwin, on what became known as 'Calamity Corner', and all except the latter were total wrecks.

With the war over, the coast of Cornwall achieved further wreck notoriety when the redundant and gunless battleship *Warspite*, on her way to the Clyde to be scrapped, decided on a less ignominious end. On 21 April 1947, the towing hawser between the old 'Queen Elizabeth' class warship and the tug *Bustler* parted when south of the Wolf Rock. For twenty-four hours the remaining tug, *Melinda III*, battled against the south-west gale, then slipped her tow, leaving the passage crew on *Warspite* no alternative but to drop an anchor. In huge seas it failed to hold, and within an hour she was ashore and stranded on Mount Mopus Ledge, near Cudden Point. At high tide, the battleship drifted off, but stranded a second time, in Prussia Cove, where it was decided she was no longer seaworthy to undertake the long tow north. She was resold where she lay. Sometime later, she was moved round to a position just west of St Michael's Mount and beached, since this gave better access during the breaking-up operation. For five years she lay there, being slowly reduced to scrap metal, the elements and the Cornish coast having inflicted more structural damage than thirty years' service, including two world wars.

Memories of the submarine accidents of the 30s were revived when in 1950 the Royal Navy lost two boats in fifteen months. The '*T*' class submarine *Truculent* had been carrying out trials following a refit at Chatham and was returning to Sheerness on the surface, when she was run down and sunk by the Swedish tanker *Divina*, on 12 January. As with the ill-fated *Thetis*, which was of the same class, the *Truculent* was over-manned, carrying a dockyard party of some eighteen in addition to her normal crew of sixty. The resultant collision was a direct result of the tanker's continuing to exhibit a single 'all-round' red light, indicating 'I am carrying explosives'. This was correct for the upper reaches of the

Thames, but not in the wide estuary or at sea. Off the Kentish Flats, the submarine's skipper assumed that it was an incorrect 'not-under-command' signal (two red lights displayed vertically one above the other), and thinking she must be anchored, he continued on course. Five minutes later, the submarine was on the bottom with a large hole in her bow. Recalling the mistakes of the *Thetis* accident, when the crew remained with the vessel so long that the majority died of anoxia, everyone aboard *Truculent* left via the escape hatch. Fifty-seven were swept away on the tide to drown or die of exposure, only fifteen being picked up alive. The wreck was subsequently salvaged, and taken to Chatham for scrapping. *Truculent* at least offered her crew some chance. HM Submarine *Affray* offered no chance at all. She submerged on 16 April 1951, and was not seen again until 14 June, and then only by means of a closed-circuit TV camera lowered to the seabed. She too carried additional personnel, twenty-three young submarine officers under training, as well as Royal Marine Commandos, due to carry out a landing exercise. The systematic search for the *Affray* was a daunting task, once it was established that she was missing, since the area to be covered represented several thousand square miles. It was also an area littered with wrecks, not only from two world wars, but also 2,000 years of civilisation. Over 200 bottom contacts had to be examined, and most of them dived on and identified, before the floodlit spectacle of *Affray*'s conning tower swam into view on a television screen. The cause of the wreck, which remains on the bottom still, is uncertain. It may have been a defect in the 'snorkel' mast, allowing the craft to flood, or it may have been something as positive and final as an internal explosion. In almost any other circumstance, surely some of the crew would have remained alive in either bow or stern compartments, and hence capable of releasing one of the two distress/marker buoys carried? The camera inspection of the hull showed both buoys still in their respective stowage.

As time passes, and with so many shipping accidents in a

lifetime, certain names bring back memories to us all, whether they be half-forgotten news headlines, something that affected us personally, or (for those more closely involved), recollections of a cold, angry sea. Over the past thirty years, although the total of annual shipwreck incidents has declined, there is still little to suggest that we are any nearer to mastering the sea, or have learnt all there is to know about ship handling and design. For 1952, possibly the best-remembered names in this context were the *Flying Enterprise* and Captain Carlson, the man who ordered forty-one crew and ten passengers to jump into the sea off Land's End in order to be saved, yet refused to leave the ship himself. He spent seven days aboard completely alone, with the deck listing at an impossible 60°, then a further six accompanied by 1st Mate Dacy of the tug *Turmoil*, until she sank beneath their feet. To the people of Liverpool, the name *Empress of Canada* brings back memories of January 1953, when the liner caught fire, and, after a spectacular blaze in Gladstone Dock, fell over on its port side. British Railways and the Transport Commission will not forget the Irish Channel passenger ferry *Princess Victoria*, nor will the relatives of the 131 who died when she foundered in a gale, that same month and year.

The sinking of the MV *Tresillian* in 1954, at the south end of St George's Channel, less than one day's sailing from her destination of Avonmouth, brought home some lessons regarding cargo stowage and ballasting that will not be forgotten. The foundering of the MV *Mitera Marigo* in Falmouth harbour in 1959 illustrated the dangers of collision. Not that collision at sea needs any publicity. In 1961 a total of 1,600 ships were involved world wide, with 1,800 the following year. There is every indication that this number will steadily rise to once again reach over 2,200, as it did in 1908 and 1929. A worrying aspect for those responsible for the operating of ships, is their ever-increasing size; whereas in the 50s a 30,000-ton tanker was 'large', by the 60s a ship of 100,000 tons was far from unusual, and this figure has now exceeded 500,000 tons! Until 1967, when the name *Torrey Canyon* became familiar to half the world, only the United States had experienced a massive oil spill, and only one ship larger than the *Torrey Canyon* had been lost at sea. Then this deep-laden tanker, bound for Milford Haven, weighing some 120,000 tons, ploughed into the Seven Stones Reef, between mainland Cornwall and the Isles of Scilly, and introduced this country to pollution on a massive scale.

Navigational problems or failure to keep a good look-out or radar watch at sea also play their part in causing shipwrecks, as the captain of the *Hemsley I* discovered in May 1969. That was when the 'oldest steamship in British register service', on her way to be scrapped, ended her days under the cliffs near Trevose Head on the north coast of Cornwall. Her Mayday signal for assistance suggested that she was ashore near the Lizard, on the opposite side of the south-west peninsula! Of the hundreds if not thousands of accidents between ships in the confines of the English Channel, especially where it narrows into the Straits of Dover, the events of January and February 1971 may never be equalled, or at least we hope not. The massive Panamanian tanker *Texaco Caribbean* sank in shallow water following collision with the *Paracas*. Within less than twenty-four hours, the motorship *Brandenburg* struck the wreck and sank, followed by the *Niki* which also went to the bottom; a fourth vessel was involved, but managed to remain afloat.

1972 saw the MV *Nefili* run headlong into the 300ft-high cliffs at Land's End to become a total wreck, *on top of the remains of an earlier coaster wreck and two steel trawlers,* all lost in the same narrow cove. The following year the petroleum-laden tanker *Dona Marika* caused concern and fears of an explosion at Milford Haven when she ran aground, and the Channel Islands assumed their own notoriety over a spate of wreck during 1973/4. It was Christmas Day 1973 when the 880ft-long, 125,000-ton super-freighter *Elwood Mead* stranded on Les Grimes Reef, off Guernsey; her cargo of iron ore alone was worth well over £10m. Miraculously she remained aground and intact until 24 February, when she was successfully refloated and saved. Other names well remembered in those years include the MV *Prosperity*, the Greek *Armas* and the tanker *Point Law*. Of these, the 2,000 ton Cypriot *Prosperity* was the worst wreck disaster in these waters since World War II. All eighteen crew members died, following an engine failure in hurricane-force winds on 16 January 1974, which hurled her on top of the La Conchée Reef, where she went to pieces.

The Seven Stones Reef was once again in the news during September 1976, when a Rumanian fish factory ship, the *Rarau*, went aground, and all eighty-four crew had to be saved when she broke in two. But the following year, 1977, was the most tragic for many a decade. *El Tambo* is a name the port authorities at Fishguard, in South Wales, will remember for many years hence. She caught fire off Strumble Head whilst carrying 900 head of Irish cattle, was towed into Fishguard harbour Roads, and eventually sank. There was a public outcry over the animals, which were removed before she went to the bottom, but the wreck is still there, awaiting dispersal. Off Cornwall, men and ships spent hundreds of hours searching for any sign of the *Union Crystal*, the *Boston Sea Ranger* and *Lady Kamilla*, all reported missing, from which there were only a total of six survivors. Since then, the Channel Islands have had the oil rig *Orion*; Cornwall the MV *Shoreham*, the *Skopelos Sky*, the *Intermac-600* and the trawler *Bounteous*. Devon claimed the coaster *Heye-P*; the *Tarpenbex* and *Aeolian Sky* sank in the Channel; the *Pool Fisher* off the Isle of Wight; the *Welfare* off Lossiemouth, and the *Athina B* off Brighton beach.

Seemingly there is no end. It is impossible to legislate against accidents, especially at sea, where weather is the predominant and uncontrollable variable. No matter how many Codes of Practice, Health and Safety Regulations, Sailing Directions and the like are produced, when things go wrong at sea, it's simply man and the ocean—as it has always been.

ACKNOWLEDGEMENTS

The bringing together of shipwreck information embracing the entire British Isles would not have been possible without the help of others, and my grateful and sincere appreciation is again extended to Eric Collins, of Penzance, whose avid reading of old newspapers continues to unearth new material. To Alec Reynolds, of the Hydrographic Department, Taunton; Will Honey, of Deal; Rex Cowan, of Hampstead; John Davis, of Truro; John Bevan, of Submex Ltd; Ken Burns, of the Plymouth Central Library (Maritime Section), and H. L. Douch, Curator of the Royal Institute of Cornwall.

Also to the staff of the Reading Room, National Maritime Museum; HM Customs and Excise Library; British Library, Reading and State Paper Rooms; Colindale Newspaper Library; Historic Manuscripts Commission; Imperial War Museum; Bodleian Library, and the St Austell (Cornwall) Public Library.

For permission to reproduce photographs or illustrations: The Trustees of the Tate Gallery; Eric Collins, Penzance; W. Honey, Deal; Richard Keen, Guernsey; C. Carter, Land's End; I. Wynne Jones, N Wales; National Maritime Museum, Greenwich; F. Gibson, Isles of Scilly; Plymouth City Library; *Illustrated London News*; *Western Morning News*; West of England Newspapers; *Daily Express*; Photographic Section, HMS *Daedalus* (SAR Flight); Studio Jon Ltd, Dyfed; H. E. Appleton, Gorleston-on-Sea RNLI; Basil James, Milford Haven; MOD(Navy).

To the late T. Stanhope Sprigg, James MacGibbon and the publishers, who have shown undeserved patience; Roy Davis and other close friends who share my enthusiasm for shipwrecks, and most of all to Bridget, for her undying support.

January 1981   *Richard Larn*

BIBLIOGRAPHY

Baptist, Capt C. N. T. *Salvage Operations*, (1979)

Barker, R. *Against the Sea*, (1972)

Barnaby, K. C. *Some Ship Disasters and their Causes*, (1968)

Barrington, G. W. *Remarkable Voyages and Shipwrecks*

Boquet, M. *Lundy Shipwrecks*, 18th annual report, Lundy Field Society, (1967)

Boulay, J. du. 'Wrecks of the Isles of Scilly', *Mariner's Mirror* reprint, vol 45, no 4, (1959) and vol 46, (1960)

Bray, J. *An Account of Wrecks*, (1759–1830), Truro, (1975)

Carter, C. *Cornish Shipwrecks—the North Coast*, Newton Abbot, (1970)

Clowes, L. W. *A History of the Royal Navy*

Colledge, J. J. *Ships of the Royal Navy*, vol I & II, Newton Abbot, (1969)

Cooke, J. H. *The shipwreck of Sir Cloudesley Shovell*, (1883)

Cooper, E. R. *Storm Warriors of the Suffolk Coast*, (1937)

Dawson, A. J. *Britain's Lifeboats*, (1923)

Edmunds, G. *The Gower Coast*, Bristol, (1979)

Everitt, D. *The K Boats*, New York, (1963)

Fallon, N. *The Armada in Ireland*, (1978)

Farr, G. *Wreck and Rescue in the Bristol Channel*, Truro, (1966)

Farr, G. *Wreck and Rescue on the Coast of Devon*, Truro, (1968)

Farr, G. *Wreck and Rescue on the Dorset Coast*, Truro, (1971)

Forsberg, G. *Salvage from the Sea*, (1977)

George, S. C. *Jutland to Junkyard*, Cambridge, (1973)

Gill, C., Booker, F., Soper, T. *The Wreck of the 'Torrey Canyon'*, Newton Abbot, (1967)

Godfrey, A., Lassey, P. *Shipwrecks of the Yorkshire Coast*, (1974)

Hadfield, R. L. *Sea Toll of Our Time*, (1930)

Hocking, C. A. *A Dictionary of Disasters at Sea in the Age of Steam, 1824–1962*, vols 1 & 2, (1969)

Hudson, K., Nicholls, A. *The Book of Shipwrecks*, (1979)

Jameson, W. *The Most Formidable Thing*, (1965)

Jefferis, R., McDonald, K. *The Wreck Hunters*, (1966)

Jones, I. Wynne, *Shipwrecks of North Wales*, Newton Abbot, (1973)

Larn, R. *Devon Shipwrecks*, Newton Abbot, (1974)

Larn, R. *Goodwin Sands Shipwrecks*, Newton Abbot, (1976)

Larn, R., Carter, C. *Cornish Shipwrecks—the South Coast*, Newton Abbot, (1969)

Larn, R. *Cornish Shipwrecks—the Isles of Scilly*, Newton Abbot, (1971)

Layson, J. F. *Memorable Shipwrecks*, London

Malster, R. *Wreck and Rescue on the Essex Coast*, Truro, (1968)

Malster, R. *Saved from the Sea*, Lavenham, (1974)

Martin, C. *Full Fathom Five*, (1975)

Mattingly, G. *The Defeat of the Spanish Armada*, (1959)

McDonald, K. *The Second Underwater Book*, (1970)

McDonald, K. *The Wreck Detectives*, (1972)

McDonald, K. *The Treasure Divers*, (1978)

McKee, A. *The Golden Wreck*, (1961)

McKee, A. *King Henry VIII's Mary Rose*, (1973)

Noall, C., Farr, G. *Wreck and Rescue round the Cornish Coast*, vols I, II & III, Truro, (1964)

Padfield, P. *An Agony of Collisions*, (1966)

Parry, H. *Wreck and Rescue on the Coast of Wales*, Truro, (1969)

Potter, J. S. *The Treasure Divers Guide*, (1973)

Rees, P. H. *Gower Shipwrecks*, Swansea, (1978)

Shaw, F. H. *Famous Shipwrecks*, (1930)

Shaw, F. H. *Full Fathom Five*, (1930)

Shipwrecks and Tales of the Sea, (1888)

Skidmore, I. *Anglesey and Lleyn Shipwrecks*, Swansea, (1979)

Smith, C. *The Men of Mumbles Head*, Llandysul, (1977)

Snyder, G. S. *The Royal Oak Disaster*, Abingdon, (1976)

Temple, C. R. *East Coast Shipwrecks*, Norwich, (1974)

Verney, Capt E. H. *The Last four days of the Eurydice*, (1878)

Wheeler, Capt G. J. *Ship Salvage*, (1958)

Wood, W. *Survivors Tales of Famous Shipwrecks*, (1932)

NEWSPAPERS, JOURNALS, ETC

Annual Register, from 1774
British Vessels Lost at Sea, vol I, 1914–18; II, 1939–45 HMSO
Burney Newspaper Collection, various 1603–1800
Calendar of Domestic State Papers; Fine Rolls State Papers; Pipe Rolls State Papers; Treasury State Papers
Catalogue of the Archives of the Confederate of the Cinque Ports & Right of Wrecks (1656)
Daily Telegraph, various issues
Deal Mercury, various issues
Deposition Books, various, HM Customs & Excise
Express Newspapers, various issues
Gentlemans Magazine, various issues
Lifeboat, Journal of the Royal National Lifeboat Institution
Lloyds Captains Registers, 1868–1947
Lloyds Casualty Returns, various issues
Lloyds Confidential Index, 1886–1920
Lloyds List, from 1743
Lloyds Marine Loss Records, 1939–1970
Lloyds Missing Vessel Books, 1873–1954
Lloyds Universal Register, various issues 1764–1980
Lloyds Weekly Shipping Index, 1880–1917
Naval Chronicles, various issues
Naval & Military Gazette, various issues
Sea Breezes, various issues 1932–1980
Sherborne and Yeovil Mercury, various issues
State Papers, various Board of Trade inquiries into losses
State Papers, Board of Trade report on Shipwrecks, 1865/74
The Morning Post, various issues
The Naval and Military Record
The Shipwrecked Mariner, various issues from 1854
The Times
The London Illustrated News, various issues
Willing's Press Guide, 81st issue

INDEX OF SHIPS

Page references in italic denote illustrations. For simplicity, where sailing ships are concerned, the abbreviation used up until the nineteenth century is 'S', after which conventional abbreviations are used for all types of vessel.

INDEX OF SHIPS

INDEX OF SHIPS

INDEX OF SHIPS

GENERAL INDEX

Page numbers in italics refer to illustrations